pocket posh® word power

120 WORDS YOU SHOULD KNOW

**Andrews McMeel
Publishing, LLC**

Kansas City • Sydney • London

POCKET POSH® WORD POWER: 120 WORDS YOU SHOULD KNOW

copyright © 2011 by Wordnik®. All rights reserved. Printed in China. No part of this book may be used or reproduced in any manner whatsoever without written permission except in the case of reprints in the context of reviews.

Andrews McMeel Publishing, LLC
an Andrews McMeel Universal company
1130 Walnut Street, Kansas City, Missouri 64106

www.andrewsmcmeel.com

11 12 13 14 15 LEO 10 9 8 7 6 5 4 3 2 1

ISBN: 978-1-4494-1461-0

Library of Congress Control Number: 2010934820

Project Editor: Angela Tung

Illustration by robinzingone®

ATTENTION: SCHOOLS AND BUSINESSES
Andrews McMeel books are available at quantity discounts with bulk purchase for educational, business, or sales promotional use. For information, please e-mail the Andrews McMeel Publishing Special Sales Department: specialsales@amuniversal.com

preface

It's nearly impossible to make it through any amount of schooling without coming across the notion that a good vocabulary is a prerequisite for success. Words are the tools of thought, and the more (and more precise) tools you have, the more elegantly constructed your thoughts can be.

Of the millions of words in the English language, which are the ones that will add the most power, range, and precision to your speech and writing? There are plenty of delightful yet useless words in English (such as borborygmus, "stomach rumbling," or wayzgoose, "an annual picnic or pleasure excursion for printers"); this book is not a collection of those.

Included here are the words used by good and careful writers, by exuberant and dashing writers, and (occasionally) by terrible and pretentious writers. The difference is that good writers take their time when adding new words to their vocabulary. They don't tackle them willy-nilly but ponder their definitions, sound out their pronunciations, and (most of all) look to other writers for examples of how best to use them; we all learn best by example.

So here you will find the words that will give you the best return for your investment of time and effort (in terms of expressiveness, erudition, and eloquence), explained not only by traditional definitions but also with examples from sources both contemporary and historical. Enjoy!

—Erin McKean, CEO, Wordnik.com

1 abrogate

/ (ab'rə-gāt,)/

verb

1 To keep clear of; avoid.

2 To abolish summarily; annul by an authoritative act; repeal. Applied specifically to the repeal of laws, customs, etc., whether expressly or by establishing something inconsistent therewith.

adjective

• Annulled; abolished.

Examples:

During the Constitution's ratification, Alexander Hamilton assured New Yorkers that the Constitution would never permit the federal government to "alter or **abrogate**" a state's "civil and criminal institutions [or] penetrate the recesses of domestic life, and control, in all respects, the private conduct of individuals." —John Yoo, "Gay Marriage: Leave It to the Voters," *The Wall Street Journal*, August 12, 2010

Still, he thought that you could probably trust Mr. Roosevelt and Comrade Stalin to **abrogate** liberty only just so much as was absolutely necessary—and always in the right direction, that is, to abrogate your opponent's liberty rather than your own. —Mary McCarthy, *The Company She Keeps*, 1939

1

Public outrage over their misbehavior was so vehement that the Senate voted to **abrogate** the company's defense contracts. —Wordnik

In law, an act of *abrogating*, or *abrogation*, can be expressed or implied. *Expressed abrogation* is more pronounced by a new law in general or particular terms; *implied abrogation* occurs when a new law contains provisions positively contrary to the former law.

2

affable
/ (af'ə-bəl)/

adjective

1 Expressing or betokening readiness to converse or be addressed; mild; benign: as an affable countenance.
2 Easy of conversation or approach; admitting others to intercourse without reserve; courteous; complaisant; of easy manners; kind or benevolent in manner; now usually applied to those high placed or in authority: as an affable prince.

Examples:

The volume trails away in **affable** narrated anecdotal sketches as if Dahl had lost interest in the craft of storytelling, as he seems to have lost the sting of vengefulness. —Joyce Carol Oates, "The Art of Vengeance," *The New York Review of Books*, April 26, 2007

"I can't say it's because I lead a particularly dark life; I lead a pretty stable life," [writer James Lasdun] says in **affable** tones from his home in Woodstock, where he lives with his wife, the author Pia Davis, and their two children. —Susan Comninos, "Author of the Anxious," *Times Union*, October 25, 2009

Erect and stiff, chest out, chin whiskers to front, eyes blinking independently, my uncle is superb. Or when he raises his hat with a large, outward gesture of his arm, bowing slightly from the shoulders, in **affable** salutation. —Alvin Johnson, "My Uncle," *American Prose Selections*, 1920

Affable is related to the word *fame* in that both share the Latin suffix *fari*, "to speak."

affect

/ (ə-fekt' *or* af'ekt)/

verb

1 To act on; produce an effect or a change on; influence; move or touch: as cold affects the body; loss affects our interests.

2 To make a show; put on airs; manifest affectation.

noun

1 Affection; passion; sensation; inclination; inward disposition or feeling.

3

2 State or condition of body; the way in which a thing is affected or disposed.
3 Emotion.

Examples:

What I do think the [new treatments] affect is the priority the public gives to the epidemic, the willingness to mobilize resources. —Arlene Getz, "The Epidemic Is Growing in Frightening Ways," *Newsweek*, July 5, 2002

There are women whom we affect to scorn with the full power of our contempt; but I doubt whether any woman sinks to a depth so low as that. She also may be a drunkard, and as such may more nearly move our pity and affect our hearts, but I do not think she ever becomes so nauseous a thing as the man that has abandoned all hopes of life for gin. —Anthony Trollope, *Orley Farm*, 1861

Affect is often used interchangeably—and incorrectly—with *effect*. *Affect* is usually used as a verb; *effect* is more often used as a noun (meaning "result or outcome"). *Affect* is what you do; *effect* is what you get.

4 alacrity

/ (ə-lak'ri-tē)/

noun

1 Liveliness; briskness; sprightliness.
2 Cheerful readiness or promptitude; cheerful willingness.
3 Readiness; quickness; swiftness.

Examples:

The young woman engaged to the man of fifty fainted half-way, and would have proceeded, but finding him wanting in **alacrity** for catching her she sat down trembling. —Thomas Hardy, *Wessex Tales*, 1888

"Certainly, Madame," said Gaston, rising with **alacrity** from the piano, and coming to the fireside; "is there anything I can do?" —Fergus Hume, *Madame Midas*, 1889

Anthony Wood met Baltzar at Oxford, and says he "saw him run up his fingers to the end of the finger-board of the Violin, and run them back insensibly, and all in **alacrity** and in very good time, which he nor any one in England saw the like before." —George Hart, *The Violin*, 1909

Our curiosity flagged, conscious as we were all the time of his unblinking ferret-eyes on us, and we showed a certain

5

alacrity to return the passport to its rightful owner. —Ruth Pierce, *Trapped in "Black Russia,"* 1918

We gave our quick and cheerful waitress a hefty tip as she served us not just with politeness but with **alacrity**. —Wordnik

It could be said that *celerity*, "rapidity of motion," is the neutral form of *alacrity*, which evokes a feeling of cheerfulness.

5

animadversion
/ (an͵ə-mad-vûr'zhən *or* an͵ə-mad-vûr'shən)/

noun
1 The act or faculty of observing or noticing; observation; perception.
2 The act of criticizing; criticism; censure; reproof.

Examples:
Ann declared the television show silly and worthless, but this **animadversion** was only based upon the commercials she had seen. —Wordnik

On Wednesday, March 31, when I visited him, and confessed an excess of which I had very seldom been guilty; that I had spent a whole night in playing at cards, and that I could not look back on it with satisfaction; instead of a harsh **animadversion**, he mildly said, "Alas, Sir, on how few things can we look back with satisfaction." —James Boswell, *The Life of Samuel Johnson*, 1791

Animadversion is related to the Latin word *animus*, meaning "spirit, temper" (especially a hostile spirit or angry temper).

6 **antediluvian**
/ (an͵ti-də-lōō'vē-ən)/

noun

1 One who is very old or very antiquated in manners or notions; an old fogy.

2 Humorously, one who lived before the deluge.

adjective

1 Existing before the flood (the Noachian deluge) recorded in Genesis; relating to the times or events before the Noachian deluge: as the *antediluvian* patriarchs: by extension, applied to the time preceding any great flood or inundation.

2 Belonging to very ancient times; antiquated; primitive; rude; simple: as *antediluvian* ideas.

Examples:

What was way back in **antediluvian** times of late 2007 and long ago 2008, an exhilarating whoosh toward a moment when we could rid ourselves of this eight-year nightmare on the wings of (take your pick) an honest-to-goodness war hero/historically positioned woman/transcendently gifted outsider, has now become a dispiriting slog through filler and gosh darn indignation. —Richard Laermer, "Can't We Get This Over with Already! A Hopeful Plea to the Electorate," *The Huffington Post*, April 29, 2008

At her new job, Sharon felt **antediluvian** amid a sea of twenty-somethings and recent college grads. —Wordnik

Antediluvian was coined by English physician Sir Thomas Browne (1605–1682).

aplomb
/ (ə-plom' *or* ə-plum')/

noun
- Self-possession springing from perfect confidence in oneself; assurance.

Examples:
Always mature for her age, [Amy] had gained a certain **aplomb** in both carriage and conversation, which made her seem more of a woman of the world than she was, but her old petulance now and then showed itself, her strong will still held its own, and her native frankness was unspoiled by foreign polish. —Louisa May Alcott, *Little Women*, 1868–1869

One firm that has handled both the original recall and last week's hybrid announcement with particular aplomb is the Cambridge, Massachusetts–based "car-sharing" company Zipcar. —"How Budget, Avis, and Zipcar Are Dealing with the Toyota Recall," *The Economist*, February 15, 2010

She had all the marvellous "aplomb" of her countrywomen, who can transgress all laws of fashion or taste, and through sheer self-confidence remain correct. —E. Phillips Oppenheim, *The Great Secret*, 1908

Don't get me wrong, there are things US movie actors do beautifully, but being weird-looking and crowbarring lines about goblins and dragons off the page with aplomb is not one of them. —Phil Hoad, "Need a Villain? Dial Ralph Fiennes," *The Guardian*, April 13, 2010

Aplomb is derived from the French phrase *à plomb*, meaning "perpendicularly" or "poised upright, balanced," and the Latin *plomb*, or "lead weight."

apogee

/ (ap'ə-jē)/

noun

1 The point in the orbit of a planet or other heavenly body that is at the greatest distance from the earth; especially, that particular point of the moon's orbit.

2 Figuratively, the highest or most distant point; climax; culmination.

Examples:

Now, the earth occupies one of the foci of the ellipse, and so at one point in its course is at its **apogee**, that is, at its farthest from the sun, and at another point it is at its perigee, or nearest to the sun. —Jules Verne, *The Mysterious Island*, 1874

For reasons related to normal rhythms of American politics and to Barack Obama's abnormal lurch to the left, his presidency probably has passed its **apogee**. —George F. Will, "Obama's Apogee in His Rearview Mirror," *Newsweek*, July 2, 2010

Apogee is derived from the old idea that the earth is the center of the universe. When it was discovered that the sun is the center, the terms *perihelion*—"the point of the orbit of a planet or comet in which it is at its least distance from the sun"—and *aphelion*—"the point of a planet's or comet's orbit that is most distant from the sun"—were used.

9 apoplectic

/ (ap͵ə-plek'tik)/

noun

- A person affected with or predisposed to apoplexy; a sudden loss or impairment of consciousness and voluntary motion, caused by the rupture of a blood vessel in the brain, an embolism, or other cerebral shock.

adjective

1 Serving to cure apoplexy: as *apoplectic* balsam.
2 Of the nature of or pertaining to apoplexy; affected with apoplexy: as an *apoplectic* fit; an *apoplectic* patient.
3 Predisposed or tending to apoplexy: as an *apoplectic* person; an *apoplectic* habit of body.

Examples:

This disease seldom requires the use of the lancet except in apoplectic cases, and it must be left to the discrimination of the physician to employ or omit this remedy. —William A. Shaw, *Lectures on the Utility of Temperance Societies*, 1832

[Katharine] Hepburn is haughty and indomitable as an overprotective mother, while [Elizabeth] Taylor is rivetingly sensual even in apoplectic fits of distress—witness the climactic flashback scene. —John Farr, "On Her Birthday, the Best Elizabeth Taylor Movies by Farr," *The Huffington Post*, February 23, 2009

The dinner, meanwhile, was moving to its triumphant close, to the evident satisfaction of Mrs. Bry, who, throned in apoplectic majesty between Lord Skiddaw and Lord Hubert, seemed in spirit to be calling on Mrs. Fisher to witness her achievement. —Edith Wharton, *The House of Mirth*, 1905

In nonmedical contexts, *apoplectic* means "extremely angry, furious."

10 apostate
/ (ə-pos'tāt, *or* ə-pos'-tit)/

adjective
- Unfaithful to religious creed or to moral or political principle; traitorous to allegiance; false; renegade: as the *apostate* lords.

noun
1 In the Roman Catholic Church, one who, without obtaining a formal dispensation, forsakes a religious order of which he or she has made profession.
2 One who is guilty of apostasy; one who has forsaken the church, sect, party, profession, or opinion to which he or she before adhered (used in reproach); a renegade; a pervert.

Examples:

An apostate is one who renounces and gives up his religion, not one who merely neglects it. —Thomas L. Kinkead, *Baltimore Catechism*, 1891

This I know to be dangerous, because a Muslim who has once been declared to be an apostate is also a person who can be sentenced to death. —Christopher Hitchens, "At the Desert's Edge," *Vanity Fair*, July 2007

But Buchanan, who considers Bush an apostate from the conservative church, still speaks of Nixon as one of the faithful. —George F. Will, "Vacuum vs. Resentment," *Newsweek*, March 9, 1992

An *apostate* may practice *apostasy* outside religion. For instance, a Republican who has become a Democrat may call himself a *political apostate*.

11 **armillary**
/ ('ärmə‚lerē)/

adjective
• Resembling a bracelet or armilla; consisting of rings or circles.

noun

- An *armillary* sphere is an instrument consisting of gradu-
ated metal circles used to represent the motions of celes-
tial bodies around the earth.

Examples:

A string of bears'-claws, tastefully arranged, encircled his
neck, while ample folds of brass wire above the wrists and
elbows furnished his armillary, and from his ears hung rude
ornaments—some of silver, others of brass or iron—cruelly
distending the flexible members that bore them. —Rufus B.
Sage, *Rocky Mountain Life*, 1857

At the same time, paving the way for Galileo, incredibly
complex Renaissance-era astrological instruments such as
armillary spheres and planetary clocks, manufactured by
the foremost goldsmiths of Europe, show the connection
between the applied arts, mathematics and technology. —
Judith Harris, "Celebrating Galileo in Florence," *California Literary Review*,
March 22, 2009

Where the four circles, the horizon, the zodiac, the equator,
and the equinoctial colure join; the last three intersecting
each other so as to form three crosses, as may be seen in the
armillary sphere. —Dante, *The Divine Comedy*, 1308–1321

Armillary comes from a Latin word meaning "bracelet" and is related to the word *armus*, which means "shoulder."

(12) **arrant**
/ (ar'ənt)/

adjective

1 Thorough; downright; genuine: in a good sense.

2 Wandering; itinerant; vagrant; errant: as a knight *arrant*; an *arrant* preacher: especially in thief *arrant* or *arrant* thief, a roving, outlawed robber; a highwayman. Now written *errant*.

3 Notorious; manifest; unmitigated; downright: in a bad sense: as an *arrant* rogue; an *arrant* coward; *arrant* nonsense.

Examples:

Jasmine should throw everything to the winds, and lose herself in **arrant** egotism once more! —Gilbert Parker, *The Judgment House*, 1913

"No; the so-called poetry you young writers are dishing out nowadays—I call it **arrant** rot!" —Knut Hamsun, *Shallow Soil*, 1913

Or another **arrant** act of aggression that has gone down the memory hole: the 1941 joint Soviet–British invasion of Iran to grab its oil, an act every bit as illegal and reprehensible as the Soviet–German joint invasion of Poland. —Eric Margolist, "Time to Face the Truth About World War II," *The Huffington Post*, September 10, 2009

But it is very clear that such a conception, if carried out consistently to extreme lengths and applied indiscriminately to everything, must result in arrant folly. —Zénaïde A. Ragozin, *Chaldea*, 1893

Arrant and *errant* are often used interchangeably when meaning "wandering" or "roving." However, *arrant* also means "downright"— genuine in a positive sense, notorious in the negative.

13 **asperity**

/ (a-sper'i-tē)/

noun

1 Roughness of surface; unevenness: opposed to *smoothness*.

2 Roughness of sound; harshness of pronunciation.

3 Harshness of taste; sourness.

4 Roughness or ruggedness of temper; crabbedness; bitterness; severity.

5 Disagreeableness; unpleasantness; difficulty.

Examples:

In the question of the grazing lands his peevish asperity is notorious and in Mr Cuffe's hearing brought upon him from an indignant rancher a scathing retort couched in terms as straightforward as they were bucolic. —James Joyce, *Ulysses*, 1922

With all its merits, there are those who have thought that there was one thing in the declaration to be regretted; and that is, the asperity and anger with which it speaks of the person of the king; the industrious ability with which it accumulates and charges upon him all the injuries which the colonies had suffered from the mother country. —Edward Sylvester Ellis, *Thomas Jefferson, a Character Sketch*, 1898

Asperity comes from the Latin word *asper*, meaning "rough," and is related to *exasperate*, "to increase in severity, to incite by means of irritation," and *aspersion*, "slander or the act of slandering."

14

atavistic

/ (ˌatə'vistik)/

adjective

1 Pertaining to or characterized by atavism, which is:

2 In biology, reversion, through the influence of heredity, to ancestral characters; resemblance exhibited by a given organism to some remote ancestor; the return to an early

or original type by its modified descendants; restoration of structural characters that have been lost or obscured.

3 In pathology, the recurrence of any peculiarity or disease of an ancestor in remote generations.

Examples:

Home butchery certainly isn't for everyone but Lamb Club members leave with a better understanding of and heightened respect for the animal, the joy of having saved a shedload of money and a certain atavistic glow of pride at carrying home a big chunk of meat to the family. —Tim Hayward, "As Cheap as Chops," *The Guardian*, November 19, 2008

Likewise, spending an hour or two wandering rows of nearly endless varieties of apple trees or a slope covered in lines of tidy blueberry bushes with the sun on your face, looking for ripe fruit with your kids, or even a date, is the kind of atavistic, wholesome good time that Wii hasn't gotten close to touching yet. —Lee Gardner, "Easy Pickings," *Baltimore City Paper*, May 20, 2009

Atavistic comes from the Latin *atavus*, "ancestor." *Atavus* is made up of *atta*, "father," and *avus*, "grandfather."

15 banal

/ (bə-nal', bā'nəl, *or* bə-näl')/

adjective

1 Common; commonplace; hackneyed; trite; stale.

2 Of or pertaining to a ban, or provincial governor: as the royal banal court at Agram.

3 Subject to manorial rights; used in common: as a banal mill or oven.

Examples:

Jean Seberg had played a most ordinary American girl in Paris, yet whereas everything about Seberg's life seemed poetic, everything about Alice's now struck her as banal.
—Alain de Botton, *The Romantic Movement: Sex, Shopping, and the Novel*, 1996

Americans mostly live in banal places with the souls of shopping malls, affording nowhere to mingle except traffic jams, nowhere to walk except in the health club. —Jerry Adler, "Bye-Bye Suburban Dream," *Newsweek*, May 15, 1995

"Some photos radiate from a center of joy and possibility, others challenge us to consider what forms hope takes in banal or desperate situations," said Paul Raushenbush, associate dean of religious life and one of the exhibition's

curators. —Eric Quiñones, "Exhibition Presents Perspectives on Hope,"
News at Princeton, December 1, 2010

Banal comes from the French *banal*, "shared by tenants in a feudal
jurisdiction"—in other words, common or communal or activities. For
instance, the *four banal* was the communal baking oven in Medieval
France.

bemused
/ (bi-myoozd')/

verb
1 Deeply absorbed in thought.
2 Perplexed by many conflicting situations or statements;
filled with bewilderment.

Examples:
The poor Eurolanders, convinced that their economies are
on the verge of a real upturn, could do nothing but watch in
bemused fashion as their currency fell to a new low against
both the dollar and the pound and also looked uncomfortably weak against the yen. —"Playing to the Crowd," *Newsweek*,
February 7, 2000

England, who had yet to win an international match all
winter, will, as Andrew Strauss said afterwards, take what
they can get and could scarcely hide their smiles as they

wandered bemused from the pitch to the dressing room. —
Mike Selvey, "England Have Last Laugh as First One-Dayer Ends in Farce,"
The Guardian, March 21, 2009

When [Sarah Palin] brought her family to the podium at the
conclusion of the deconstruction of Barack Obama and Joe
Biden that was little short of vivisection, Democrats who
had expected to roll their eyes in bemused disbelief instead
shook their heads in admiration. —Wesley Pruden, "A Live Dream
for Hillary's Women," *The Washington Times*, September 5, 2008

Bemused is sometimes used to mean "with amused confusion."

canard
/ (kə-närd')/

verb

1 To imitate or produce the peculiar harsh cry of the duck,
   as an unskilled player on a wind instrument.
2 To fly or float about, or circulate as a canard or false report: as certain stories *canarding* about the hotels.

noun

• An absurd story or statement intended as an imposition; a
  fabricated story to which currency is given, as by a newspaper: a hoax.

Examples:

To the surprise of nobody who saw through the "free market" canard from the beginning, the overarching theme of conservatism today is to heap blame for the sinking vessel anywhere but upon where it belongs—itself. —Rob Warmowski, "A Year in David Mamet's Marketplace," *The Huffington Post*, March 11, 2009

The birth-certificate canard is just the latest version of those campaign-year attempts to strip Obama of his American identity with faux controversies. —Frank Rich, "Small Beer, Big Hangover," OpEdNews.com, August 2, 2009

Canard means "duck" in French. The meaning "an absurd story, a hoax" probably comes from the phrase *vendre un canard à moitié*, meaning literally "to sell half a duck," or "to swindle."

18 **chicanery**

/ (shi-kā′nə-rē *or* chi-kā′nə-rē)/

noun

• Mean or petty artifices; trickery; sophistry.

Examples:

Jonas's cynical partner . . . falls for the upstanding local sheriff (Liam Neeson) who's out to expose Jonas, and is transformed by the love of a good man. And Jonas, confronted with a crippled boy of true faith (Lukas Haas), suddenly after years of chicanery is stricken with a dubious attack of conscience. —David Ansen, "Not a Season to Be Jolly," *Newsweek*, December 28, 1992

To secure such a wholesale aggrandizement he had been unscrupulous in chicanery, sleepless in his aggression, ruthless to the extremest verge of cruelty; no treaty had been too solemn to tear up, no oath too sacred for violation, no act of blood too pitiless. —Hamilton Drummond, *The Justice of the King*, 1911

Chicanery, upon a small scale, and in a miserable dark office, is a degradation; but the delicate and elaborate chicanery of politics, by which a statesman is enabled to outwit parties, or deceive whole nations, is a masterpiece of human talent! —George William McArthur Reynolds, *The Mysteries of London*, 1846

Chicanery comes from the French *chicanerie*, "trickery," and *chicaner*, "to quibble."

19 **chimera**

/ (kī'mirə *or* kə'mirə)/

noun

1 In Greek myth, a fire-breathing monster, the forepart of whose body, according to the *Iliad*, was that of a lion, the middle that of a goat, and the hinder that of a dragon, or that, according to Hesiod, had three heads, one of each of these animals: supposed by the ancients to represent a volcanic mountain of that name in Lycia, the top of which was said to be the resort of lions, the middle that of goats, and the foot that of serpents. The Chimera, a symbol of storms and other destructive natural forces, was overcome and slain by the hero Bellerophon.

2 In ornamental art, a fantastic assemblage of animal forms so combined as to produce a single complete but unnatural design.

3 An absurd or impossible creature of the imagination; a vain or idle fancy; a fantastic conceit.

Examples:

As a common name "chimera" is used by Milton to denote a terrible monster, and is now current (in an age which rejects such fabulous creatures) in the sense of a wild fancy; hence the adj. *chimerical* = wild or fanciful. —John Milton, *Milton's Comus*, 1891

My dear friend, I wish you would abandon this vain chimera of your imagination, and let common sense and reason convince you of the folly of this mad rebellion. —Henry C. Watson, *The Old Bell of Independence*, 1851

Chimera comes from the from the Greek word *khimaira*, meaning "she-goat."

20 **comity**
/ (kom'i-tē)/

noun

1 Mildness and suavity in intercourse; courtesy; civility.
2 In international law, the courtesy between states or nations by which the laws and institutions of the one are recognized, and in certain cases and under certain limitations given effect, by the government of the other within its territory.

Examples:
The privilege of a recognized foreign State to sue in the courts of a foreign State upon the principle of comity is recognized by both International Law and American Constitutional Law. To deny a sovereign this privilege "would manifest a want of comity and friendly feeling." —*The Constitution of the United States of America: Analysis and Interpretation*, 1953

There may well be occasions in which a degree of bipartisan comity is useful but it's hard to see why tinkering with health insurance is one of them. —Alex Massie, "Happy New Year!" *The Spectator*, December 31, 2009

The punishment for such comity is Tea Party declarations of being a traitor: witness Lindsey Graham's second censure this week by a South Carolina County Republican Party for his bi-partisan work on climate change. —Jay Newton-Small, "Senate Retirements Point to Dems' Uphill Election Fight," *Time Magazine*, January 7, 2010

The *comity of nations* is courteous respect between nations for each other's laws and institutions.

21 **contretemps**

/ (kon'trǝ-tän, *or* kôn,trǝ-tän')/

noun

1 An unexpected and untoward event; an embarrassing conjuncture; a hitch.

2 In music, same as syncopation.

Examples:

It's a conversational novel, roving and inclusive, packed with Southern color and Northeastern grit, with rueful reflection and the contretemps of daily life that can't be avoided even on a remote island in the Puget Sound. —Liesl Schillinger, "Objects in the Mirror," *New York Times*, September 25, 2009

The only contretemps of any great importance which occurred in the whole neighbourhood, was the unexpected arrival of a guest at the house of Mr. Stephens. —Frances Trollope, *Young Love*, 1844

Contretemps may also refer to a fencing blunder or a compound step in ballet.

contumely

/ (kon'tōō-mə-lē, kon'tyōō-mə-lē, *or* kon'-təm-lē)/

noun

1 Insolently offensive or abusive speech; haughtiness and contempt expressed in words; overbearing or reviling language; contemptuousness; insolence.
2 A contumelious statement or act; an exhibition of haughty contempt or insolence.

Examples:

The malice of contumely is not, of course, equal in all cases; circumstances have a great deal to do in determining the gravity of each offense. —John H. Stapleton, *Explanation of Catholic Morals*, 1904

He set to this work not only the inhabitants of the island (because they should not think it done in contumely and despite) but also all his own soldiers. —Sir Thomas More, Utopia, *The Harvard Classics*, 1909–1914

The girls known as the Group demonstrated such expert contumely that no outsiders dared approach them for fear of even one harsh look. —Wordnik

Although *contumely* ends in *-ly*, it is not an adverb. It is derived from the Old French word *contumelie*, meaning a reproach or insult.

23

cynosure

/ (sī'nə-shoor͵ *or* sin'ə-shoor͵)/

noun
• Something that strongly attracts attention; a center of attraction.

Examples:
His brother is physically more gifted—strong, handsome, charming—a cynosure. —Joseph Epstein, "A Yiddish Novel with Tolstoyan Sweep," *The Wall Street Journal*, February 7, 2009

But the real cynosure of the occasion last August was the smiling, snowy-haired man who is the bride at every wedding and the corpse at every funeral he attends, the 42nd president of the United States, Bill Clinton. —Todd S. Purdum, "The Comeback Id," *Vanity Fair*, July 2008

Where there is no love lost between two people, there is no chance of a human child being born into this world and the child is always the cynosure of parental care and beauty. —Kamaru Zzaman, "Human Cloning and Its Social Impacts," *Ground Report*, January 14, 2008

Cynosure comes from the Latin *cynosura*, literally "dog's tail" but also the former name of the constellation Ursa Minor. *Cynosura* also refers the constellation's brightest star, Polaris, or the North Star, used as a center of navigation.

24 deliquesce

/ (del͵i-kwes')/

verb

1 To liquefy or melt away gradually, as part of the normal process of growth: said of certain tissues, especially the gills of fungi.
2 To melt or dissolve gradually, or become liquid by absorbing moisture from the air, as certain salts do; to melt away.

Examples:

The old local order has been broken up or is now being broken up all over the earth, and everywhere societies deliquesce, everywhere men are afloat amidst the wreckage of their flooded conventions, and still tremendously unaware of the thing that has happened. —H. G. Wells, *A Modern Utopia*, 1905

The word "Ice-Cream" was no sooner whispered than it passed from one to another all down the tables. . . . Its appearance had been deferred for several reasons: first, because everybody would have attacked it, if it had come in with the other luxuries; secondly, because undue apprehensions were entertained (owing to want of experience) of its tendency to deliquesce and resolve itself with alarming rapidity into puddles of creamy fluid; and, thirdly, because the surprise would make a grand climax to finish off the banquet. —*The Atlantic Monthly*, April 1860

In gemology, the study of gems, the opposite of *deliquesce* is *effloresce,* "to become a powder by losing water to the exposed air."

25 desuetude

/ (des'wi-tōōd, *or* des'wi-tyōōd,)/

noun

- Discontinuance of use, practice, custom, or fashion; disuse: as many words in every language have fallen into desuetude.

Examples:

It is true, the fashion of wearing the collar, whether gold or silver, may be said to have been in desuetude for centuries.
—"Collar of SS," *Notes and Queries*, August 24, 1850

Flanking the path (which varies in width along the meandering nine-block route now open, up to West 20th Street) are planting beds meant to evoke the lush, self-sown greenery that thrived on the High Line during its three decades of desuetude. —Martin Filler, "Up in the Park," *The New York Review of Books*, August 13, 2009

Conventional wisdom in Indonesia holds that the monument's decline came with Java's conversion to Islam in the 1400s, but by then the great stone lotus had long since fallen into desuetude. —Jaime James, "Borobudur, Path to Enlightenment," *The Wall Street Journal*, September 13, 2008

Despite the fact that slide projectors had long since fallen into desuetude, David still insisted on using one, much to the amusement of his audience. —Wordnik

Laws and legislation may fall in *desuetude* if not enforced for a long period of time.

26 desultory

/ (des'əl-tôr,ē, des'əl-tōr,ē, *or* dez'-əl-tōr,ē)/

adjective

1 Veering about from one thing to another; whiffling; unmethodical; irregular; disconnected: as a desultory conversation.

2 Leaping; hopping about; moving irregularly.

3 Coming suddenly, as if by leaping into view; started at the moment; random.

4 Swerving from point to point; irregularly shifting in course; devious: as desultory movements; a desultory saunter.

Examples:

Though his aims were desultory, Fitzpiers's mental constitution was not without its admirable side; a keen inquirer he honestly was, even if the midnight rays of his lamp, visible so far through the trees of Hintock, lighted rank literatures of emotion and passion as often as, or oftener than, the books and materiel of science. —Thomas Hardy, *The Woodlanders*, 1887

As an accompaniment to their labours, in desultory fashion, they kept alive the embers of a facetious wrangling argument—their respective vocabularies, albeit more or less ensanguined, exhibiting a fluent and masterly range of

32

quaint barrack-room idiom and invective. —Ralph S. Kendall, *The Luck of the Mounted*, 1920

Forgetting everything he had learned at school, he spent his intervals of toil in **desultory** amusements, or in pursuing his own shadow upon the hills. —Charles Rogers, *The Modern Scottish Minstrel*, 1886

Desultory is related to *desultor*, "a bareback rider in the Roman circus who rode two or more horses at once, leaping from one to another."

27

effete

/ (i-fēt')/

adjective

1 Spent, worn out.
2 Marked by self-indulgence, triviality, or decadence.
3 Overrefined; effeminate.

Examples:

Unless the heart were truly that fountain where life and heat are restored to the refrigerated fluid, and whence new blood, warm, imbued with spirits, being sent out by the arteries, that which has become cooled and **effete** is forced on, and all the particles recover their heat which was failing, and their vital stimulus wellnigh exhausted. —William Harvey, *On the Motion of the Heart and Blood in Animals*, 1628

I am sunk deep here, in effete Manuscripts, in abstruse meditations, in confusions old and new; sinking, as I may describe myself, through stratum after stratum of the Inane, down to one knows not what depth! —Ralph Waldo Emerson, *The Correspondence of Thomas Carlyle and Ralph Waldo Emerson, 1834–1872*, 1883

Calling her a "scrappy blue-collar mama" in contrast to a more "effete" Obama, Dowd writes that "one of the most valuable lessons the gritty Hillary can teach the languid Obama—and the timid Democrats—is that the whole point of a presidential race is to win. —Stephen Schlesinger, "Maureen Dowd Likes Hillary," *The Huffington Post*, April 2, 2008

Effete comes from the Latin word *effetus*, "worn out, exhausted," formed by the prefix *ex*, "out," and *fetus*, "bearing young."

egregious
/ (i-grē'jəs *or* i-grē'-jē-əs)/

adjective

1 Extreme; enormous (usually in a bad or derogatory sense).
2 Above the common; beyond what is usual; extraordinary. In a good sense, distinguished; remarkable.

Examples:

But by far the most egregious is the use of Duran Duran's "Hungry Like the Wolf" during the trailer; Simon, Nick, John—how could you let this happen? —Jen Chaney and Liz Kelly, "From 'Kitty Galore' to 'Yogi Bear': Vote for the Most Horrific Family Movie Trailer," *The Washington Post*, July 29, 2010

What makes the Senate action particularly egregious is the fact that the United States Supreme Court, in "Citizens United vs. Federal Election Commission," is seriously considering doing away with restrictions on corporations and unions giving unlimited funds to political campaigns based on free speech protections. —David Jones, "Philanthropy Turns Away from Aggressive Advocacy for the Poor," *The Huffington Post*, September 24, 2009

And lastly and most egregious is the notion that Obama's race is somehow giving him an unfair advantage with his supporters. —Eric Kleefeld, "Hillary's New Mississippi Ad: She's a Comeback Kid," *TPM Election Central*, March 10, 2008

Egregious is derived from the Latin phrase *ex grege*, "rising above the flock," and is related to *gregarious*, "disposed to live in flocks or herds" or "sociable," derived from the Latin for "belonging to a flock."

29 **enervate**

/ (en'ər-vāt,)/

verb

1 Figuratively, to deprive of force or applicability; render ineffective; refute.
2 To deprive of nerve, force, or strength; weaken; render feeble: as idleness and voluptuous indulgences enervate the body.
3 To cut the nerves of.

adjective

• Weakened; weak; enervated.

Examples:

But within a few days, apparently, of this date treatment employed on the advice of Dr. Joshua Ward, so weakened a body already "enervate" and emaciated, that at first the patient "was thought to be falling into the agonies of death."
—G. M. Godden, *Henry Fielding: A Memoir*, 1909

For, in the constitution of man, abstinence [from food] may enervate, weaken, and kill. And there are many other ills, different from those of repletion, but no less dreadful, arising from deficiency of food. —Hippocrates, *On Ancient Medicine*, 5th Century B.C.

For great empires, while they stand, do enervate and destroy the forces of the natives which they have subdued, resting upon their own protecting forces; and then when they fail also, all goes to ruin, and they become a prey. —Francis Bacon, *The Essays*, 1601

If any method could be devised to enervate the English colonies it would be to establish in them the Inquisition. —Voltaire, A *Philosophical Dictionary*, 1764

Enervate comes from the Latin *enervare*, "weaken," or literally "cut the sinews of."

30 epiphany
/ (i-pif′ə-nē)/

noun

1 A manifestation or appearance of a divine or superhuman being.
2 An illuminating realization or discovery, often resulting in a personal feeling of elation, awe, or wonder.
3 Season or time of the Christian church year from the Epiphany feast day to Mardi Gras (Shrove Tuesday), the day before Ash Wednesday, the start of Lent.

Examples:

An epiphany, in its strictly religious sense, is when the Divine reveals something to a person (or to humanity). In a more secular sense . . . an epiphany is a sudden realization. Of the big picture. Of something hidden. Of the missing puzzle piece. Of clarity in the midst of chaos. —Cathleen Falsani, "Epiphany: Celebrating Moments of Truth," *The Huffington Post*, January 6, 2009

The problem with John [McCain]'s epiphany is not that he saw the light, he saw the presidency slipping from his grasp. —"Britain Moves to Prop Up Country's Banks; Presidential Debate: McCain, Obama Trade Jabs; McCain's Math Problem: Needs to Win Over Independents," *CNN Transcripts*, October 8, 2008

Whether the Davos crowd took our advice or had an independent epiphany is hard to say, but they have made good use of the free time between ski seasons to improve their methodology. —"Davos Epiphany," *The Wall Street Journal*, November 1, 2007

Epiphany comes from the Greek word *epiphainesthai*, meaning "to appear, manifest, or show."

(31) errant
/ (er'ənt)/

adjective

1 Wandering; roving; rambling: applied particularly to knights (knights errant) of the Middle Ages, who are represented as wandering about to seek adventures and display their heroism and generosity.
2 Deviating; straying from the straight, true, or right course; erring.

Examples:

"Ah, señor," here exclaimed the niece, "remember that all this you are saying about knights-errant is fable and fiction; and their histories, if indeed they were not burned, would deserve, each of them, to have a sambenito put on it, or some mark by which it might be known as infamous and a corrupter of good manners." —Miguel de Cervantes, *Don Quixote*, 1616

The problem is that the increasing size of files, such as video, has begun overwhelming some equipment handling the traffic, resulting in errant or lost packets. —Bobby White, "Its Creators Call Internet Outdated, Offer Remedies," *The Wall Street Journal*, October 2, 2007

She spends her spare time worrying about terrorists using errant nuclear material from aging reactors to make bombs.
—Wordnik

Errant and *arrant* are often used interchangeably when meaning "wandering" or "roving." However, *arrant* also means "downright"—genuine in a positive sense, notorious in the negative.

32

ersatz
/ (er'zäts, *or* er-zäts')/

adjective
- Made in imitation; artificial, especially of an inferior quality.

noun
- Something made in imitation; an effigy or substitute.

Examples:
Based on everything I've read, seen, and heard, as black gay male, a member of the upper middle class, a college-educated white collar worker, and a non-Christian and non-theist. . . . I am one of the most irrelevant, least important voters in this election. I am also not a "real American" living in the "real America." At best, I am an "ersatz American." —Terrance Heath, "Observations from an Ersatz American," *The Huffington Post*, October 27, 2008

On each weekly edition of this latest ersatz "reality" hour, the gigantic Robbins—who's sold, you know, a jillion books and already devoured hundreds of hours of TV time—tries to extend his domain further by playing pop shrink to sundry souls in distress. —Tom Shales, "Sorry, Tony Robbins. Your 'Breakthrough' Has a Much Bigger Problem to Fix," *The Washington Post*, July 27, 2010

Not that long ago, corporate Japan still functioned as a kind of ersatz welfare state, with companies offering their workers so-called lifetime employment with ample benefits. —Christian Caryl, "The Gap Society," *Newsweek*, November 3, 2007

Ersatz comes from the German word ersetzen, meaning "to replace."

execrable

/ (ek'si-krə-bəl)/

adjective

1 Deserving to be execrated or cursed; very hateful; abhorred; abominable: as an execrable wretch.
2 Very bad; intolerable: as an execrable pun.
3 Piteous; lamentable; cruel.

Examples:

At last, after an endless interval, someone approached with a deliberate, shuffling tread, the door was unbarred—there seemed several bolts—and opened half-way to reveal a gim-crack interior in execrable taste and the figure of an old woman with a hard wrinkled face and grey hair smoothly banded under a black cap. —Alice Campbell, *Juggernaut*, 1929

[The road] is in execrable condition. . . . It is all knocked to pieces with traffic, and frequently pitted with shell holes, and as a rule very narrow. —Innes Logan, *On the King's Service*, 1817

The powdered head of the old man appeared at the window of the chaise, and the Swiss of the embassy replied, in execrable French, to a question put to him thus: "Monsieur, the Marquis de Maulear does not stop in the embassy. His apartments were too small for two." —"The Count of Monte-Leone: Or, The Spy in Society," *The International Monthly*, April 1851

Synonyms for *execrable* include *flagitious*, *villainous*, *nefarious*, *cursed*, *accursed*, *detestable*, and *odious*.

34

extempore
/ (ik-stem'pə-rē)/

adjective

1 On the spur of the moment; without previous study or preparation; offhand: as to write or speak extempore.
2 Extemporary; extemporaneous.

noun
- Language uttered or written without previous preparation.

Examples:

The gift of composing poetry extempore is given to very few, yet it is human. —Baruch Spinoza, *The Theologico-Political Treatise*, 1670

But to let mere lads speak extempore is to give rise to the acme of foolish talk. —Plutarch, *Plutarch's Morals*, 1898

In late years, when Harcourt had to pilot his famous Budget through Committee, he acquired a perfect facility in extempore speech; but at the beginning it was not so. —George William Erskine Russell, *Fifteen Chapters of Autobiography*, 1860

While the bass sustained the melody, the other voices indulged in extempore descant (*composizione alla mente*) and in extravagances of technical execution (*rifiorimenti*), regardless of the style of the main composition, violating time, and setting even the fundamental tone at defiance. —John Addington Symonds, *Renaissance in Italy*, 1887

"The sooner the better," said the Queen: and she then most fervently engaged in extempore prayer. —"Death of Queen Caroline," *The Mirror of Literature, Amusement, and Instruction*, May 5, 1832

Extempore comes from the Latin phrase *ex tempore*, meaning "of time."

(35) **facetious**
/ (fə-sē'shəs)/

adjective
1 Treating serious issues with deliberately inappropriate humor; flippant.
2 Pleasantly humorous, jocular.

Examples:
The "Merchant" and the "Shipman" may indulge in facetious or coarse jibes against wives and their behaviour, but the "Man of Law," full of grave experience of the world, is a witness above suspicion to the womanly virtue of which his narrative celebrates so illustrious an example, while the "Clerk of Oxford" has in his cloistered solitude, where all womanly blandishments are unknown. —Sir Adolphus William Ward, *Chaucer*, 1880

He told her that such misrepresentations were quite possible, and that they embodied a form of humour which was getting more and more into vogue among certain facetious persons of society. —Thomas Hardy, *A Laodicean: a Story of To-day*, 1881

The friends of the new knight were inclined to banter him, and proposed his health at a dinner in facetious terms. — George William Erskine Russell, *Collections and Recollections*, 1898

The name, incidentally, has inspired some hardcore snark from a number of writers, who seem blissfully unaware that the term has long been in facetious use in scientific circles to describe the critical element that is just beyond reach. —William Bradley, "The Common Threads of *Avatar*," *The Wall Street Journal*, December 22, 2009

Facetious and *sarcastic* may seem like synonyms. However, *facetious* has lighter connotations and comes from the French word *facétieux*, meaning "jest," whereas *sarcastic* is more scornful and biting, coming from the Greek word *sarkazein*, meaning "to bite the lips in rage."

36

facile

/ (fas'əl)/

adjective

1 Easy to be done, performed, or used; easy; not difficult.
2 Easy to be moved, removed, surmounted, or overcome.
3 Easy to access or converse with; affable; not haughty, austere, or reserved.
4 Easily moved or persuaded to good or bad; pliable; flexible; yielding.

5 Ready; quick; dexterous: as a *facile* artisan or artist; he wields a *facile* pen.

Examples:

Messer Andrea could say things with a certain facile grace that kept them from rankling, and at the moment the utterance of this truth was of consequence. —Mrs. Lawrence Turnbull, *The Royal Pawn of Venice*, 1911

They were thus engaged in facile talk when Albert de Chantonnay emerged from the long window of his study, a room opening on to a moss-grown terrace, where this plotter walked to and fro like another Richelieu and brooded over nation-shaking schemes. —Henry Seton Merriman, *The Last Hope*, 1904

The sketches themselves, invented by a top-notch six-person cast under the guidance of Napier and musical director Ruby Streak, are clever, provocative, and notably lacking in facile mockery. —Albert Williams, "Not Just Funny," *Chicago Reader*, January 6, 2005

Today *facile* may imply the idea of being too easy, lazy, or simplistic and has the archaic definition of being "mild in a pleasant way."

37

factitious
/ (fak-tish'əs)/

adjective
1 Created by humans, artificial.
2 Counterfeit, fabricated.

Examples:
Spencer criticizes this conception of Hobbes as representing society as a "**factitious**" and artificial rather than a "natural" product. —Washington Allston, *Lectures on Art*, 1850

No rubbishy pseudobooks, no selling of tickets in advance, no attempts at a **factitious** excitement. —John Russell, "Islamic Treasures on View at the Met," *The New York Times*, November 20, 1981

The doctrine, it is to be observed, which is expanded through many pages of the book on Original Sin, is not merely that men are legally guilty, as being devoid of "true virtue," though possessed of a certain **factitious** moral sense, but that they are actually for the most part detestably wicked. —Sir Leslie Stephen, *Hours in a Library*, Volume I, 1892

Certainly, the reader can do without it: the Hell that Mr. Jones writes about is terrible enough without bringing in **factitious** echoes of Dante. —Bernard Bergonzi, "Out Our Way," *The New York Review of Books*, January 20, 1966

Synonyms for *factitious* include *artificial*, *unnatural*, *plastic*, and *synthetic*.

farrago
/ (fə-rä'gō *or* fə-rā'gō)/

noun
• A mass composed of various materials confusedly mixed; a medley; a hodgepodge.

Examples:

Another more elaborate prescription consists of a long list of ingredients, including burnt sponge, saponaria, the milk of a sow raising her first litter, with numerous simple herbs, and the sole object for which this nonsensical farrago is introduced here is to add that both these prescriptions are copied from the surgery of Roger. —Henry Ebenezer Handerson, *Gilbertus Anglicus*, 1918

Posner reviews them all in turn, in a hectic flurry of piled-up fact-bites, speculative calculations, passing quarrels, and off-hand policy dicta—an orderless mixture of assertion, guess, remark, and opinion for which the term "farrago" would seem to have been invented. —Clifford Geertz, "Very Bad News," *The New York Review of Books*, March 24, 2005

Their lyrics (punctuated by nutty shouts of "yeah, yeah, yeah!") are a catastrophe, a preposterous **farrago** of Valentine-card romantic sentiments. —Jesse Larner, "Cultural Reactionaries," *The Huffington Post*, January 21, 2008

Farrago comes from the Latin word *farrago*, meaning "mixed fodder for cattle" or "mixture." *Farrago* is related to *farina*, "a fine flour or meal made from cereal grains."

39

fatuous
/ (fach'o͞o-es)/

adjective

1 Foolish; foolishly conceited; feebly or stupidly self-sufficient; unconsciously silly: applied both to people and to their acts.
2 Idiotic; demented; imbecile.
3 Unreal; illusory, like the *ignis fatuus*.

Examples:

I will not call it **fatuous**, inane, and exasperating vanity or self-absorption; I will put it in the form of a parable. —Hilaire Belloc, *The Path to Rome*, 1916

Secondly there are plenty of men who under the pressure of fashion devote much effort to the improvement of their form in **fatuous** sports, which otherwise applied would go a considerable way in the improvement of their minds and in widening their range of interests. —W. Bateson, "The Place of Science in Education," *Cambridge Essays on Education*, 1919

In *The Third Policeman*, the narrator's one great comfort in the endless doom of the afterlife, in which he will forever be arriving in a demented Irish village ruled by policemen who are both godlike and **fatuous**, is sleep. —Fintan O'Toole, "Oblomov in Dublin," *The New York Review of Books*, August 13, 2009

Fatuous comes from the Latin word *fatuus*, meaning "foolish." *Ignis* (Latin for "fire") *fatuus* is "a meteoric light that sometimes appears in summer and autumn nights and flits in the air a little above the surface of the earth, chiefly in marshy places, near stagnant waters, or in churchyards." The *ignis fatuus* is also called will o' the wisp.

(40) **feckless**
/ (fek'lis)/

adjective
1 Lacking purpose.
2 Without skill, ineffective, incompetent.
3 Lacking the courage to act in any meaningful way.
4 Lacking vitality.

Examples:

It is said that he had an uncle, a clever active mechanic, who could do many things with his hands, and contemplated James's indolent, dreamy, "feckless" character with impatient disgust. —John Hill Burton, *The Book-Hunter*, 1882

By "feckless" . . . [my sister] means I didn't graduate from an Ivy League school (she went to Smith); I'm not married (any more); I have not raised a family, nor do I have plans to in the immediate future (see *not married*); I don't own a house (life-long renter) or even a car; and I don't have a job (belletrist). —August Kleinzahler, "Diary," *London Review of Books*, February 11, 2010

Mr. Bernanke's former Princeton University colleague, Nobel laureate Paul Krugman, has become the loudest critic of Mr. Bernanke's inaction, calling the Fed "feckless" (lacking in vitality, unthinking, irresponsible) in his *New York Times* column. —David Wessel, "The View from Bernanke's Perch at the Fed," *The Wall Street Journal*, July 21, 2010

Feckless has a Scottish origin. The word *feck*, meaning "power, force, strength," is an alteration of "effect."

41 fiduciary

/ (fi-dōō'shē-er̩ē, fi-dōō'shə-rē, fi-dyōō'shə-rē,
or fī-dyōō'shə-rē)/

adjective

1 Confident; steady; undoubting; unwavering; firm.
2 Having the nature of a trust, especially a financial trust;
   pertaining to a pecuniary trust or trustee: as a *fiduciary*
   power.

noun

• One who holds a thing in trust; a trustee.

Examples:

The Senate bill to authorize County Treasurers and other
county officers, and other persons holding Confederate
Treasury Notes in fiduciary capacity, to dispose of them under the recent legislation of Congress, and for other purpos-
es, was read the first time. —*Journal of the House of Representatives of
the State of Mississippi*, 1864

Several of the studies focus on proposals that are vigorously
opposed by banking industry groups or Wall Street firms,
like a change that would make stock brokers subject to the
same fiduciary standards as financial advisers—that is, to
act in the best interest of their customers. —Edward Wyatt, "As

ies," *The New York Times*, March 16, 2010

Most borrowers were not first time homeowners and trusted the professionals to play it straight, as in "fiduciary responsibility." —Iris Martin, "Homeowner, Don't Let the Wolf in Your Door!" *The Huffington Post*, April 3, 2009

Fiduciary comes from the Latin word *fīdūcia*, meaning "trust," and is related to *fidelity* and *faith*.

foment

/ (fō-ment')/

verb

- To encourage; abet; instigate or promote by incitement: commonly used in a bad sense: as to *foment* discord.

Examples:

Alcohol and a heated argument were enough to foment a brawl among the partiers. —Wordnik

So far, experts say that the discontent pooling on the right (anti-Washington and anti–Wall Street) and to a lesser degree on the left (anti–Wall Street) has some, but not yet all, of the ingredients needed to foment radicalism. —Clay Waters,

"NYT Ponders: Weather Underground, Tea Party Movement Just 'Varying Degrees of Rage,'" *The Wall Street Journal*, March 30, 2010

Mankind, it seems, is beset with plenty of inherent evil and requires no outside agency to **foment** more. —George Loomis, "Better the Devil You Don't Know?" *The New York Times*, March 3, 2010

The difference between the figurative senses of *foment* and *ferment* is subtle: *Foment* means "to encourage," or to warm up something that has already started, whereas *ferment* means "to set in agitation," or to start the hubbub.

43

garrulous
/ (gar'ə-ləs *or* gar'yə-ləs)/

adjective
- Given to talking much and with much minuteness and repetition of unimportant or trivial details.

Examples:
He walked back with the young men, prattling to them in **garrulous** good-humour, and making bows to his acquaintances as they passed; and thinking innocently that Pen and George were both highly delighted by his anecdotes, which they suffered to run on in a scornful and silent acquiescence.
—William Makepeace Thackeray, *The History of Pendennis, His Fortunes and Misfortunes, His Friends and His Greatest Enemy*, 1901

He thought of Heath sitting by the bed of the dying woman, and he thought of him following the wake of the *Lady Helen* down the dark river with sad, sorrowful eyes, and through the thought there came a strange thrill to his own soul, because he touched the hem of the garment of the Everlasting Mercy, hidden away, pushed out of life, and forgotten in **garrulous** hours full of idle chatter. —Marjorie Douie, *The Pointing Man*, 1920

Davis, who's soft-spoken yet **garrulous**, is always either on the phone, coordinating deliveries and orders from suppliers, or gabbing with customers. —Grant Pick, "Stayin' Alive," *Chicago Reader*, November 16, 2000

Garrulous comes from the Latin word *garrīre*, meaning "to chatter." Synonyms include *talkative, prating, loquacious, prattling, babbling, chatty,* and *gabby*.

44

gauche
/ (gōsh)/

adjective
• Awkward or lacking in social graces; bumbling.

Examples:
In its evolution from a physical description to a social one, louche is reminiscent of its French cousin **gauche**, which

literally means "left," as in "left-handed." —Nancy Friedman, "Word of the Week: Louche," *Fritinancy*, June 7, 2010

What distinguishes a witty or tactful performance from one that was clumsy or gauche is some mental act which renders it witty, tactful, or the lack of such, which renders it clumsy or gauche. —"Gilbert Ryle," *Stanford Encyclopedia of Philosophy*, December 18, 2007

Withers hangs his head, appalled at this gauche and obsequious question. —Alix Sharkey, "Bill Withers Interview," *Telegraph*, August 10, 2010

Condescending public displays of noblesse oblige don't impress me. They strike me as new-money gauche, like some parvenu dentist who gives a few bucks to the local art museum and then sends a news release about it to the local paper. —Andy Obermueller, "It's Time to Take Buffett's Millionaire Challenge," *Street Authority*, August 6, 2010

Some low-end joints may do it on the sly, but generally speaking, it's a no-no, and it would be considered terribly gauche to ask to take leftovers home in a nicer establishment, anyway. —Ruth Brown, "Diary of an Immigrant," *Willamette Week*, August 9, 2010

In French, *gauche* also means "left." In the past, left-handed people were thought to be clumsy and awkward.

gestalt
/ (gə'sh-tält *or* gə'sh-tōlt)/

noun
- A collection of physical, biological, psychological, or symbolic entities that creates a unified concept, configuration, or pattern that is greater than the sum of its parts (of a character, personality, or being).

Examples:
Even if you don't blame McCain, per se, for the Wall Street meltdown this weekend, there is no getting around the fact that the Republican Party mania against the federal regulatory agenda protecting consumers and workers has been part of the McCain gestalt from the time he was first elected to Congress. —Howie Klein, "Who Wants to Extend and Deepen the Bush Economic Miracle?" *The Huffington Post*, September 16, 2008

Another perceptual trait found in language is the gestalt or recognized whole. In music, for example, we can hear a melody and recognize it again even when the melody is played in a different key and at a different tempo. Visually, objects retain a recognizable consistency despite changes in input. . . . The most famous gestalt is our capacity to perceive a series of separate still photographs as continuous motion when the pictures are shown rapidly enough. —Edmund Blair Bolles, "What I've Learned About Language," *Babel's Dawn*, September 14, 2008

Gestalt has German origins and is the past participle form of the German verb *stellen*, "to place."

46 hauteur
/ (hō-tûr')/

noun
• Haughty feeling or bearing; arrogant manner or spirit.

Examples:

A haughty young lady in the dining-room, Birdie Callahan, in her stiffly starched white, but beneath the icy crust of her **hauteur** was a molten mass of good humor and friendliness. —Edna Ferber, *Fanny Herself*, 1917

She recalled his **hauteur** and studious coldness towards herself, his air of deep understanding and mastery, his magic look of wizardly youth, his eloquence, his immense self-possession, his mysterious connection with Cleopatra's indisposition and recovery. —Anthony M. Ludovici, *Too Old for Dolls*, 1921

The ambassador has not the least German stiffness or hauteur; is extremely civil, and so domestic a man, that he talked comfortably of his wife and eight children, and of his fondness for them. —Horace Walpole, *The Letters of Horace Walpole, Earl of Orford*, 1842

So what's good about "The Addams Family"? Ms. Neuwirth, for openers, whose cool, leggy hauteur is impossible to resist. —Terry Teachout, "I've Seen That Show Before," *The Wall Street Journal*, April 9, 2010

Hauteur is derived from the French word *haut,* meaning "high." *Haute couture* is a common term for "high fashion" or "any unique stylish design made to order for wealthy and high-status clients."

47

hegemony

/ (hi-jem'ə-nē *or* hej'ə-mō͵nē)/

noun

- Predominance; preponderance; leadership; specifically, headship or control exercised by one state over another or others, as through confederation or conquest: originally applied to such a relation often existing between the states of ancient Greece.

Examples:

America has never been an empire, it has never pursued an overtly imperial policy, and even its global hegemony is of a very peculiar kind, much less effective and much more fragile than commonly thought. —Steven Levingston, "America as a New Rome?" *The Washington Post*, April 15, 2010

Yet a leftish middle-class hegemony is far from the whole story; the area has always had a strong working-class presence that has uneasily coexisted alongside its louder and newsier monied neighbours. —John Crace, "The London Comprehensive That's Schooled Labour's Elite," *The Guardian*, August 2, 2010

On our continent, it is far easier to grasp lost hegemony from a Mexican or Native American viewpoint. —Jim Luce, "Tibet: Polar Perspectives. Can Both Be Heard?" *The Huffington Post*, April 20, 2009

Commercial media hype to distract us from conglomerate owned media's mission of war-mongering, support for empire and predatory global financial hegemony is obvious, insensitive and inappropriate to our mourning the passing of a fellow human being. —Jay Janson, "Cronkite Belatedly Called War in Vietnam Unwinnable, Not an Atrocity," OpEdNews.com, July 19, 2009

Hegemony comes from the Greek word *hēgemōn*, meaning "leader."

48 homologous

/ (hə-mol'ə-gəs *or* hō-mol'ə-gəs)/

adjective

1 Having the same relative position, proportion, value, or structure; having correspondence or likeness.
2 Showing a degree of correspondence or similarity such that it suggests a common origin.
3 Corresponding to a similar structure in another life form with a common evolutionary origin (e.g., flippers and hands).

Examples:

Geoffroy St-Hilaire has strongly insisted on the high importance of relative position or connection in homologous parts; they may differ to almost any extent in form and size, and yet remain connected together in the same invariable order. —Charles Darwin, *The Origin of Species*, 1859

For the evolutionist, the statement that two structures are homologous is the result of a great deal of theory building. —Philip P. Wiener, *Dictionary of the History of Ideas*, 1973

In general, it may be stated that the members of an homologous series show a regular gradation in most physical properties and are similar in chemical properties. —William Edwards Henderson and William McPherson, *An Elementary Study of Chemistry*, 1905

There are technologies presented to the Efe on a regular basis, as well as various cultural "traits" from which they can pick and chose. And they do. The analogous and possibly homologous Pygmies of the western part of Central Africa took on Portuguese crossbows. —Greg Laden, "Why Did the Tasmanians Stop Eating Fish?" *Culture as Science—Science as Culture*, August 8, 2010

Homologous is opposed to *heterologous*, "having different relationships or different elements" or "relating to different species."

hubris

49

/ (hyo͞o′bris)/

noun

1 Excessive pride, presumption, or arrogance (originally toward the gods).
2 Unchecked arrogance.

Examples:

For an industry supposedly based on serving consumers' credit needs, their hubris is awe-inspiring as the banks and their hired guns set out to take down the proposed Consumer Financial Protection Agency—the best thing going for consumers in the Obama Administration's regulatory reform agenda that's now being considered in Congress. —

Tram Nguyen, "Don't Let Bankers Gut the Consumer Protection Agency," *The Huffington Post*, August 6, 2009

Some of the projects featured on the show seem like exercises in hubris—Singapore, do you really need a 7,000-ton "sky park," 650 feet in the air, linking the tops of three skyscrapers? —Rachel Saslow, "'Build It Bigger' Airs on Science Channel; Museum Portrays Eskimo Tools," *The Washington Post*, May 11, 2010

The display of raw colonialist hubris is so pronounced that locals now refer to U.S. ambassador Hugo Llorens as "the proconsul." —Mary Anastasia O'Grady, "The U.S. vs. Honduran Democracy," *The Wall Street Journal*, March 29, 2010

Obviously the conservative movement is intoxicated with hubris right now. Part of this hubris is their belief that the American people are truly and deeply on their side and that the last two elections were either a fluke or the product of a GOP that was too centrist. —Jonathan Chait, "Tactical Radicalism and the End of the GOP Establishment," *The New Republic*, July 18, 2010

Hubris comes from the Greek word *hybris*, meaning "insolence."

hypotenuse

/ (hī-pot'n-ōōs, *or* hī-pot'n-yōōs,)/

noun
• The side of a right triangle opposite the right angle.

Examples:
"That the square of the hypotenuse is equal to the squares of the two sides" is a proposition which expresses a relation between these figures. —Sir John Alexander Hammerton and Arthur Mee, *The World's Greatest Books*, 1910

Some New York citizens, often just after meeting you, will immediately ask how you got there and what route you took. "I took a cab," I say. To which they reply: "Oh you could have just taken the N train to 14th street and then walked three blocks east to Lexington, or you just walk to 12th and University and take a cab from there up Broadway because it'll save you time, it's like a hypotenuse, then walk four blocks past the National Arts Club to Madison Square Park and pick up a rickshaw from there down to 28th street" —Jonathan Daniel Harris, "What I Love and Hate About New York," *The Huffington Post*, August 8, 2009

The glass on the sliding door had an uncleaned film in each corner like a right triangle with a concave hypotenuse where the rag hadn't quite gotten into the corner. —Larry Strattner, "The Sex Life of Your Mouth," *Fictionaut*, May 2010

Hypotenuse comes from the Greek word *hupoteinein,* meaning "to stretch or extend under," and is part of the Pythagorean theorem, which states that "the square of the length of the hypotenuse of a right triangle is equal to the sum of the squares of those of the other two other sides."

51 **implacable**
/ (im-plak'ə-bəl *or* im-plā'kə-bəl)/

adjective

1 Not placable; not to be appeased; not to be pacified or reconciled; inexorable: as an implacable prince; *implacable* malice.

2 Not to be relieved or assuaged.

Examples:
But yet it becomes them that see their state, and that their day is coming, to pity and bewail their condition, yea, and to pray for them too; for who knows whether it is determined that they should remain implacable to the end, as Herod; or whether they may through grace obtain repentance of their doings, with Saul. —John Bunyan, *Works of John Bunyan*, 1872

These words fell one after the other slowly and gravely, with a certain implacable rhythm, like the strokes of the axe upon an oak-tree. —Victor Hugo, "Ninety-Three," *Great Sea Stories*, 1921

Eventually, the couple agreed to settle their divorce out of court, but the two men remain implacable enemies. —Richard Kay, "Spencer's Ex Finally Gets Her Divorce," *Daily Mail*, June 4, 2009

Duvall, craggy and implacable, is Felix Bush, a backwoods hermit who—after 40 years of self-imposed exile—rides into town one day in the late 1930s to arrange his own "living funeral." —Ella Taylor, "'Get Low': Greeting Death with a Deadpan Smirk," NPR, July 29, 2010

Synonyms for *implacable* include *relentless, inexorable, unappeasable, unforgiving, vindictive, pitiless,* and *rancorous.*

52 **imply**
/ (im-plī') /

verb

1 To express in a suggestive manner rather than as a direct statement.
2 To have as a necessary consequence.
3 To suggest a logical inference.

Examples:

What, after all, does "democratic cultural education" mean? What I think you imply is that, if we taught art and music appreciation in the schools, more people would appreciate art and music. —Glenn Kurtz, "Who Cares About Classical Music, Part Two," *The Huffington Post*, June 4, 2007

But I think I still have to go with it being more a matter of there actually being a pretty constant stream of election poll results showing Senator Clinton in the lead, that election poll results are generally regarded as news and Election Central (as the name might imply) is an election news aggregator. —Eric Kleefeld, "Poll: Hillary Running Well Against Republicans in Missouri," *TPM Election Central*, October 20, 2007

The laws also frustrate reintegration, for [what] they imply is that an ex-offender can never be a full citizen. —David Cole, "Can Our Shameful Prisons Be Reformed?" *The New York Review of Books*, November 19, 2009

Imply and *infer* are often confused. Whereas *imply* means "to suggest an idea," to *infer* means "to conclude by reasoning." A speaker *implies* a meaning, and the listener *infers* a conclusion.

53 **incendiary**

/ (in-sen′dē-er‚ē)/

adjective

1 Causing or adapted to cause combustion; used in starting a fire or conflagration; igniting; inflammatory.

2 Pertaining or relating to or consisting in malicious or criminal setting on fire or burning.

3 Tending to excite or inflame passion, sedition, or violence.

noun

1 A person who maliciously sets fire to a house, shop, barn, or other inflammable property; one who is guilty of arson.

2 One who or that which excites or inflames; a person who excites antagonism and promotes factious quarrels; a violent agitator.

Examples:

Do they ever pause to reflect what would be their own feelings if, far and wide throughout their country, the ancestral hall, the farmer's homestead, and the labourer's cot were giving shelter to the licentious soldiers of an invader or crackling in incendiary flames? —Belle Boyd, *In Camp and Prison*, 1865

I believe we can thank Galliano for this lukewarm mess. Pretty young men with weird pinkish skull caps wearing garters

68

and stockings in incendiary colors. —"Senseless Trend: Men with No Pants," *The Bosh*, February 1, 2009

The same kind of incendiary rhetoric that Dutch journalists used against Fortuyn can now be seen in American left-wing coverage of any nonsocialist European party or politician. —Bruce Bawer, "Heirs to Fortuyn?" *The Wall Street Journal*, April 23, 2009

Incendiary comes from the Latin *incendium*, "fire," and is related to *incense*, "a perfume often used in the rites of various religions," or "to anger or infuriate."

54

inchoate
/ (in-kō'it)/

adjective

1 Recently started but not fully formed yet; just begun; only elementary or immature.

2 Chaotic, disordered, confused; also, incoherent, rambling.

noun

• A beginning, an immature start.

Examples:
When inchoate is used in the sense of "confused, disordered, entangled" by even fairly learned colleagues (with, however, usually no Latin and less Greek), there must be some sort of

semantic blend that imparts the sense of chaotic and adds it to the meaning "incipient." —*Verbatim: The Language Quarterly,* Vol. VII, No. 3

[Filmmaker Stanley] Kubrick dreamed of villains like this: nerds in fleece, controlling the information, calling their cult a family. It was an image, a kind of inchoate anxiety about the future, rather than anything you could put your finger on. —Vanessa Grigoriadis, "Do You Own Facebook—Or Does Facebook Own You?" *San Francisco Sentinel,* April 8, 2009

In the Chronicle of Higher Education, commentator Sasha Abramsky recently denounced Tea Partiers for "representing little more than an inchoate rage against the zeitgeist." —Eric Felton, "Where Is the Outrage?" *The Wall Street Journal,* July 16, 2010

Inchoate contains the Latin root *cohum,* meaning "strap from yoke to harness."

55 **indolent**
/ (in'də-lənt)/

adjective

1 Habitually lazy, procrastinating, or resistant to physical labor.

2 Inducing laziness (e.g., *indolent comfort*).

3 Causing little or no physical pain; progressing slowly; inactive (e.g., of an ulcer).
4 Healing slowly.

Examples:

The usual place of rendezvous for the indolent is the king's tent; where great liberty of speech seems to be exercised by the company towards each other; while in speaking of their chief they express but one opinion. —Mungo Park, *Life and Travels of Mungo Park in Central Africa*, 1840

He idled away weeks and months in indolent enjoyment in the country; he indulged his passion for the theater when opportunity offered; and he began to be weary of a society which offered little stimulus to his mind. —Charles Dudley Warner, *Washington Irving*, 1881

The blood of his folk, that had somehow seemed to stay about his heart in indolent clots, began to course to every extremity, and gave his brain a tingling clarity, a wholesome intoxication of the perfect man. —Neil Munro, *Doom Castle*, 1900

Indolent comes from the Latin *indolent*, "painless," and may have come to mean "lazy" because pain also means "labor, exertion, endeavor," as well as "unease, mental or bodily distress."

56 | ineluctable
/ (in¸i-luk'tə-bəl)/

adjective
• Impossible to avoid or escape.

Examples:
The book acknowledges the running contradictions—the lurches between poverty, sentimentality and fascism; the hypocritical entanglements of church and state; the ineluctable twinning of politics and economics. —Frank Delaney, "Five Best," *The Wall Street Journal*, March 13, 2010

Through a pale morning's arctic sunlight glinting dimly off the snow, a bank of violas emits one endless shrill note which eventually becomes electronically distorted by points of ice panning back and forth through the space between your ears, descending and then impossibly ascending in volume and ineluctable intensity until they're almost un-bearable though infinitely graceful in their beauty; at length they wind off into the skies trailing away like wisps of fading beams. —James Wolcott, "The Haunting Cheekbones of Hallowed De-spair," *Vanity Fair*, March 18, 2007

Courtney's remarks demonstrate in no uncertain terms that Congress has nothing short of an ineluctable moral obli-gation to provide the American people with quality, affordable healthcare. —Kit Gallant, "Congressman Courtney Issues Wake-Up Call to House: 'Take a Look at Yourselves in the Mirror,'" *The Huffington Post*, July 15, 2009

Synonyms for *ineluctable* include *inescapable, irresistible, inevitable, unavoidable,* and *fateful.*

57

infer
/ (in-fûr')/

verb

1 To bring in, on, or about; lead forward or advance; adduce.

2 To form as an opinion or belief in consequence of something else observed or believed; derive as a fact or consequence, by reasoning of any kind; accept from evidence or premises; conclude.

3 To bear presumption or proof of; imply.

4 To conclude; reach a conclusion by reasoning.

Examples:

Just as someone who encounters Socrates in conversation should sometimes be puzzled about whether he means what he says (or whether he is instead speaking ironically), so Plato sometimes uses the dialogue form to create in his readers a similar sense of discomfort about what he means and what we ought to infer from the arguments that have been presented to us. —"Plato," *Stanford Encyclopedia of Philosophy*, September 17, 2009

Meaning is something we infer from the experience of being alive that makes it feel worthwhile. —Ian Gurvitz, "10 Wrong Questions and False Arguments That Frame Our Thinking About Religion," *The Huffington Post*, July 23, 2010

Infer and *imply* are often confused. Whereas *imply* means "to suggest an idea," to *infer* means "to conclude by reasoning." A speaker *implies* a meaning, and the listener *infers* a conclusion.

58

internecine
/ (in͵tər-nes'ēn͵, in͵tər-nes'-in, *or* in͵tər-nē'sīn͵)/

adjective

1 Mutually destructive; most often applied to warfare.
2 Characterized by struggle within a group, usually applied to an ethnic or familial relationship.

Examples:

But the weak point of the Berber race has been its lack of homogeneity; it has ever been split up into independent states and tribes, constantly indulging in internecine warfare. —Budgett Meakin, *Life in Morocco and Glimpses Beyond*, 1905

The interior of the Carolinas was a region where neighbors, during the Revolution, engaged in internecine conflicts of Tories against Whigs. —Frederick Jackson Turner, *The Frontier in American History*, 1921

Brian Doherty's history of the American libertarian movement, *Radicals for Capitalism*, is too long and gets bogged down in internecine minutiae at times but it's still packed with goodies and is a bracing, necessary reminder that there's more to life than the Elephant and the Donkey. — Alex Massie, "Seeing Out the Old Year with the Church of Scotland," *Spectator*, December 31, 2007

Internecine comes from the Latin word *internecare*, with *inter-* as an intensive prefix and *necare*, a form of *nex*, or "death." However, in his 1755 *Dictionary of the English Language*, Samuel Johnson misinterpreted *inter-* to mean "between, mutual," resulting in the modern meaning of the word.

inveterate
/ (in-vet'ər-it)/

adjective
1 To make inveterate; render chronic; establish by force of habit.
2 Old; long established.

3 Firmly established by long continuance; deep-rooted; obstinate: generally, though not always, in a derogatory sense.

4 Confirmed in any habit; having habits fixed by long continuance: applied to people.

5 Malignant; virulent; showing obstinate prejudice.

6 Habitual, hardened.

Examples:

The Æquans accordingly sought aid from the Volscians of Ecetra; which being granted readily, (so keenly did these states vie in **inveterate** hatred against the Romans,) preparations for war were made with the utmost vigour. —Titus Livius, *The History of Rome*, 1853

So **inveterate** is our habit of criticism, that much of our knowledge in this direction belongs to the chapter of pathology. —Ralph Waldo Emerson, *Beauty*, 1860

She was one of that peculiar class of females, who, if there is any thing to be said, always claim the privilege of saying it; in other words, an **inveterate** talker; and who, if we may be allowed the phrase, managed her husband, and all around her, with the length of her tongue. —Emerson Bennett, *Ella Barnwell*, 1853

Inverarate comes from the Latin word *inveterari*, meaning "to grow old," The word is related to *veteran*, "grown old in service."

 **ironic**

/ (ī-ron'ik)/

adjective

1 Pretending ignorance; simulating lack of instruction of knowledge.

2 Both coincidental and contradictory in a humorous or poignant and extremely improbable way.

Examples:

It's actually a deceptively sprightly and at times very humorous score, employing lots of pizzicato, frequently playing in *ironic* counterpoint to what is actually unfolding in the story. —William Bradley, "The Ghost(s): Of Tony Blair, Roman Polanski, and a War on Terror," *The Huffington Post*, March 22, 2010

"I got the job done. I wish I had done it with less carnage," Troy Duffy said of his first experience in moviemaking. "That's what this time is about—doing a good job with less carnage." His words are kind of *ironic* from a guy who wrote and directed two Hub-set big-screen shoot-'em-ups that revel in high body counts. —Troy Duffy, "The 'Saints' March Back," *The Boston Globe*, October 25, 2009

In an ironic twist, Iran appears to have arrested a trio of passionate young Americans who espouse some of the same causes as Iran itself, particularly taking a stand against United States and Israeli aggression. —Danna Harman, "In Ironic Twist, Iran Detained US Hikers Critical of Israel and America," *The Christian Science Monitor*, July 30, 2010

Ironic is often used to mean simply any kind of coincidence, but actually it means having the opposite outcome from what is expected.

(61) **jejune**
/ (jə-jōōn')/

adjective

1 Scantily supplied or furnished; attenuated; poor.
2 Barren; unfurnished; lacking pith or interest, as a literary production; devoid of sense or knowledge, as a person; dry; uninteresting; shallow.

Examples:

Yet ironically, two television programs aimed at young people and animated by a kind of **jejune** foolery—Jon Stewart's *Daily Show*, and Stephen Colbert's *Colbert Report*—sell a great many books, more perhaps than more traditional "adult venues," and far more than newspaper reviews. —Benjamin R. Barber, "Doing Colbert (and Being Done by Him!)," *The Huffington Post*, April 11, 2007

To superficial observers, or observers who have convinced themselves that high lights and bright colourings are of the essence of the art of the prose writer, Clarendon may seem tame and **jejune**. He is in reality just the contrary. —George Saintsbury, *A History of Elizabethan Literature*, 1920

However, music reviewer Richard Carter wrote in *The Washington Post* that the combination of traditional and classical music "simply does not add up to anything more than a work of banal, dreary, **jejune**, prosaic vapidity." — Emma Brown, "David Fanshawe, 68, Dies; Ethnomusicologist Who Composed 'African Sanctus,'" *The Washington Post*, July 13, 2010

Jejune comes from the Latin word *ieiūnus*, "meager, dry, fasting."

62

lackadaisical
/ (lak͵ə-dā'zi-kəl)/

adjective
• Sentimentally woebegone; languid; listless; affected.

Examples:
In recent days, a host of voices (Republican and Democratic alike) began speaking out more forcefully with concern that the administration had taken a seemingly "**lackadaisical**" approach towards containing and cleaning up the Gulf spill.

—Sam Stein, "Robert Gibbs Defends White House on Oil Spill Response," *The Huffington Post*, May 23, 2010

Ashe spikes the notion that he's "**lackadaisical**" in his very first paragraph: "No matter what I do, or where or when I do it, I feel the eyes of others on me, judging me." —David Gates, "Advantage, Mr. Ashe," *Newsweek*, June 21, 1993

During the week of Nov. 23, [Arianna Huffington] called the president, one of the hardest working presidents in history, "**lackadaisical**," which, to black people, who know the dog whistles, means lazy. —Ishmael Reed, "The Selling of 'Precious,'" *Counter Punch*, December 4–6, 2009

Lackadaisical is a long word with a longer etymology. It's an extension of *lackadaisy*, which has the same meaning and is an alteration of *lackaday*, "an exclamation of sorrow or regret." *Lackaday* is also alteration of *alack the day*, which itself is an alteration of *alas the day*, combining "alas" and "alack." *Alas* comes an Old French phrase, *a las*, meaning "ah (I am) miserable," and *lack* comes from Middle Dutch *lac*, "deficiency, fault."

63 laconic
/ (lə-kon'ik)/

adjective

- Expressing much in few words, after the manner of the ancient Laconians; sententious; pithy; short; brief: as a laconic phrase.

Examples:

In order that the boys should be taught to behave well under all circumstances, they were never allowed to speak except when spoken to, and then their answers were expected to be as short and exact as possible. This style of speaking, where much was said in few words, was so usual in the whole country of Laconia, that it is still known as the laconic style. —H. A. Guerber, *The Story of the Greeks*, 1896

Hyneman sports a handlebar mustache, wears a beret and speaks in laconic murmurs, as if he's trying hard not to get too worried about the fireball likely to erupt from their latest contraption. —"Dumb Stunts, Smart Show," *Newsweek*, November 13, 2003

If you talked of books, he settled for you, in laconic sentences, works of acknowledged merit—put down men of uncontested superiority—but women of title and tainted reputation, if they would but ask him to their parties, became at once his favourites and his oracles. —"Sketches of Italy—Lucca," *Blackwood's Edinburgh Magazine*, November 1845

Laconic comes from *Lakōn,* the region of Greece of which Sparta is the capital. Spartans had a reputation for brevity of speech.

laissez-faire
/ (lesā 'fâr *or* ˌlezā 'fâr)/

noun

- A letting alone; noninterference with individual freedom of action; the let-alone principle or policy in government and political economy. The term was first used in France to designate the principle of political economy that would leave industry and trade free from taxation or restriction by government except as required by public peace and order. It has since been extended to include noninterference by controlling authority with any guiltless exercise of individual will.

Examples:

But she does look upon the current **laissez-faire** approach to penmanship with a certain dismay. —"Handwriting Is on the Wall," *The Wall Street Journal*, January 24, 2009

Their support for Polanksi demonstrates a **laissez-faire** attitude toward forbidden behavior, and it is precisely this casual approach to sensitive issues of decency that has a great many Americans outraged. —"Polanski Shocker: Rich People Are Sexual Deviants!" *Vanity Fair* Daily, October 13, 2009

If government wishes to alleviate, rather than aggravate, a depression, its only valid course is laissez-faire—to leave the economy alone. —Murray Newton Rothbard, *America's Great Depression*, 2000

Laissez-faire comes from the French word *laisser*, "to let, allow," and *faire*, "to do."

65 lugubrious
/ (loo-gōō'brē-əs *or* loo-gyōō'-brē-əs)/

adjective

1 Characterized by or expressing mourning or sorrow; mournful; doleful; funereal; dejected: as *lugubrious* wailing; a *lugubrious* look or voice.

2 Exciting mournful feelings; pitiful; dismal; depressing: as a *lugubrious* spectacle or event.

Examples:

"Well, this is a delightful ending to our picnic," said Mr Moynham in lugubrious tones, as we all lay on the ground, with the exception of the guides, who appeared to mingle freely with the robbers, who were grouped in picturesque

83

attitudes around us, leaning on their carbines. —John C.
Hutcheson, *Tom Finch's Monkey*, 1886

He lay there in **lugubrious** state, the rosy face stained with
much crying, just showing above the edge of the counter-
pane; his tangle of yellow curls crushed upon the bolster.
—Anonymous, *Choice Readings for the Home Circle*, 1916

At his best, in projects that move along at a faster pace than
he does, [Harrison Ford] comes off as a reliable Boy Scout.
As a romantic leading man in **lugubrious** soap operas, he's
as rigid and wooden as a cypress log. —Rex Reed, "What Han
Solo Had Is Now Gone: Crucifixion of a Cross-Dresser," *The New York
Observer*, October 10, 1999

Synonyms for *lugubrious* include *sorrowful, melancholy, doleful,
mournful, dismal, gloomy, woeful, pitiable,* and *depressed.*

Machiavellian
66
/ (mak̪ē-ə-vel'ē-ən)/

adjective
• Attempting to achieve their goals by cunning, scheming,
  and unscrupulous methods.

Examples:

Mr Dillon, at a later stage, with a certain **Machiavellian** cunning, raised the cry of "Unity" from every platform in the country against those who had never acted a disloyal part in all their lives, whilst his own political conscience never seemed to trouble him when he was flagrantly and foully defying that very principle of unity which he had pledged himself to maintain and uphold "in or out of Parliament." —D. D. Sheehan, *Ireland Since Parnell*, 1921

Mr. Ichiro Hatoyama had been falsely accused by certain **Machiavellian** elements in the then political establishment and had been purged the day he was to take up the position of the first elected post-war Prime Minister in 1946. —Sunil Chacko, "Japan's New Era," *The Huffington Post*, September 5, 2009

The lies were told because the end always justifies the means in **Machiavellian** schemes. —Georgianne Nienaber, "Baghdad on the Bayou: Final Report on Deception and Diaspora in New Orleans," OpEdNews.com, February 17, 2008

Machiavellian comes from Niccolò Machiavelli, a fifteenth- and sixteenth-century Italian politician and author of *The Prince,* a treatise on government in which political morality is disregarded and tyrannical methods of rule are inculcated.

67 Manichean

/ (man̦i-kē'ən)/

adjective

- Of or relating to Manicheanism, a dualistic philosophy dividing the world between good and evil principles or regarding matter as intrinsically evil and mind as intrinsically good.

Examples:

Rudy Giuliani, John McCain, and Mitt all take the prize for the "America without guilt" syndrome, which sees everything in **Manichean** terms, enabling one to blame malevolent foreigners for whatever goes wrong in the world. —Philip Giraldi, "Reinventing Terrorism for Prime Time," *The Huffington Post*, June 11, 2007

Presenting the tale in **Manichean** terms, it depicts a government so corrupt, so crushing it barely bothers hiding its assassinations, sometimes doing them right in the open. —Matt Prigge, "Formosa Betrayed," *Philadelphia Weekly*, March 30, 2010

This is not true, and if one takes it to be the case then one falls immediately into the kind of **Manichean** interpretation of the Western metaphysical tradition on which Heidegger rests his call for "destruction" (Professor Skinner's milder "deconstruction"). —Robert R. Sullivan, "Not Greek to Them," *The New York Review of Books*, November 5, 1981

Manicheanism is also "a syncretic, dualistic religion that combined elements of Zoroastrian, Christian, and Gnostic thought" and comes from the religion's founder, Iranian prophet Mani.

68 matutinal

/ (mə-tōōt'n-əl, mə-tyōōt'-n-əl, *or* mach͵oo-tī'nəl)/

adjective

- Pertaining to the morning; coming or occurring early in the day: as a *matutinal* bath.

Examples:

Mrs. Lendon's habits made it easy for her to be present in **matutinal** bloom at the young man's hasty breakfast, and she sent a particular remembrance to Lady Agnes and (when he should see them) to the Ladies Flora and Elizabeth. —Henry James, *The Tragic Muse*, 1921

The next morning Rastignac woke late and stayed in bed, giving himself up to one of those **matutinal** reveries in the course of which a young man glides like a sylph under many a silken, or cashmere, or cotton drapery. —Honoré de Balzac, *Study of a Woman*, 1904

Now, I am quite willing to admit that there are many who derive great benefit from their early morning swim, their **matutinal** walk, or their tennis before breakfast. But it should be distinctly borne in mind that there are others with whom such early morning exercise does not agree. —Philip E. Muskett, *The Art of Living in Australia*, 1893

We were able to sleep in the open air, and rose refreshed and healthy each morning, to enjoy our **matutinal** bath in the sea; and by the time the sun had risen we were engaged in various preparations for our departure for the interior. — Henry Morton Stanley, *How I Found Livingstone*, 1890

Matutinal comes from the Latin *mātūtīnus*, "of the morning," and *Matuta*, "goddess of dawn."

69

maudlin
/ (môd'lin)/

adjective

1 Tearful; lachrymose; weeping.

2 Overemotional; sickly sentimental; foolishly gushing.

3 Tipsy; fuddled; foolish from drink.

Examples:

Mary Magdalene inspires, these women say, because she was not a weakling—the weeping Magdalene whose name begat the English word "**maudlin**"—but a person of strength and character. —Barbara Kantrowitz, "The Bible's Lost Stories," *Newsweek*, December 8, 2003

She felt that if she allowed herself any softness or yielding at this moment she would spoil her spotless record of self-control and weep in **maudlin** fashion in Becky's arms. —Temple Bailey, *The Trumpeter Swan*, 1920

The beast of a man she might have come to call by that sacred name, would now be beside the snowy cot, weeping in **maudlin** rejoicing over his new treasure, if the mother had not resolutely put him away some six months before. —Eugenia Dunlap Potts, *Idle Hour Stories*, 1909

I observed a few sorry wastrels leaning in **maudlin** helplessness upon the bar as I pressed in, still cleaving to their trough—but Geordie was not among them. —Robert E. Knowles, *St. Cuthbert's*, 1905

The last day of the fortnight he came home without the waistcoat: whether he had sold that, or given it away in **maudlin** generosity, or lost it in some fantastic fashion she could never gather. —M. Leonora Eyles, *Captivity*, 1920

Maudlin is an alteration of the name of Mary Magdalene, a sorrowfully penitent disciple of Jesus.

89

70 **métier**

/ (meˈtyā *or* ˈmeˌtyā)

noun

- Trade; profession; with reference to literature or art, one's particular kind or line of ability.

Examples:

Making big shots feel comfortable in their thin skin—rather than getting under it—is Seacrest's **métier**. —Lacey Rose, "Ryan Seacrest: The Man Without a Shtick," *Forbes*, June 28, 2010

[Roman Polanski's] preferred **métier** is imagined horror; he wants us to feel as his characters feel, to fear as they fear, and as such, he doesn't torture us with props or makeup or convenient, short-hand symbols of terror, but with inference, with pictures of what we cannot see. —Sam Wasson, "Knife in the Auteur," *The Huffington Post*, January 6, 2010

While Jonathan felt his proper **métier** was lyric poetry, his parents pressured him into attending medical school. —Wordnik

At boarding school, Rufus, fooling around at the piano, discovered his **métier**. —Jim Windolf, "Songs in the Key of Lacerating," *Vanity Fair*, May 22, 2007

Métier means "trade, profession" in French.

90

71 **mien**
/ (mēn)/

noun

- A person's air, manner, or expression of countenance;
look; bearing; appearance; carriage.

Examples:

The excellency of the figure and mien of the young Sieur
De Croix, was at that time beginning to draw the attention
of the maids of honour towards the terrace before the palace
gate, where the guard was mounted. —Laurence Sterne, *The Life
and Opinions of Tristram Shandy, Gentleman,* 1904

Characters pleased with themselves please others, for they
are joyous and natural in mien, and are at liberty from
thinking of themselves to pay successful attention to others.
—"Our Monthly Gossip," *Lippincott's Magazine,* August 1878

At that psychological moment an elderly man of buxom
build, benevolent in mien, and with smooth, long hair that
had an upward rolling tendency at the ends, looked in the
shop as he was passing. —Belle Kanaris Maniates, *Amarilly of Clothes-
line Alley,* 1915

I know in my life, when I was first entering this business,
coming into the room and having long blonde hair and a

long face and sort of serious **mien** . . . that defined me for many, many people. —Juliet Chung, "Mastering the Art of Partnerships," *The Wall Street Journal*, July 25, 2009

Mien is an alteration of the Middle English *demeine*, "demeanor," which is from the Old French *demener*, "to behave."

72

mirabile dictu
/ (mi-rä‚bi-lē dik'tōō)/

adjective
• Wonderful to relate.

Examples:

But now, **mirabile dictu**, her publisher, W. W. Norton, has remedied this situation and made Instead of a Letter available for a new generation of readers. —Nancy Pearl, "Library Nancy Pearl Picks 'Under the Radar' Reads," NPR, August 3, 2010

Inside, the scene is equally unorthodox, with an open kitchen, simple slate floors and even—**mirabile dictu**—an extremely friendly waiter. —Catherine Nixey, "French Cuisine: Putting the Feel-Good Factor Back into Food," *Telegraph*, August 6, 2010

The Mets had actually come back from a 6 run deficit to tie the game up. **Mirabile dictu!** It's a miracle! —Paul J. Nebenfuhr, "The Road Less Traveled," *MLB Center*, August 1, 2010

They were running the ball from inside their own twenty-five—not because of some new-found "confidence" but because Graham Henry et al figured out that, **mirabile dictu**, if you keep the ball in hand, you can score tries and win the game. —Jeremy Gordin, "Why the Springboks Are So Bad," *Politics Web*, July 21, 2010

Mirabile dictu is a direct translation from Latin. *Mīrābilis* means "wonderful," and *dīcere* means "to say."

73

misnomer
/ (mis-nō'mər)/

noun

1 A misnaming; the act of applying a wrong name or designation.
2 A mistaken name or designation; a misapplied term.

verb

• To designate by a mistaken or unsuitable name; misname.

Examples:

The facts are now known to us far more extensively than he could know them, and the adjective "unconscious," being for many of them almost certainly a **misnomer**, is better replaced by the vaguer term "subconscious" or "subliminal."— William James, *The Varieties of Religious Experience*, 1929

93

Carriers across Asia are surprising investors with losses stemming from fuel-hedging programs. The misnomer is that all of these are "hedges," when some are merely soured bets on oil. —Mohammed Hadi, "Airlines Get Caught with Hedges Down," *The Wall Street Journal*, November 29, 2008

Fortune online is calling Apple's new commercials for Face-Time "heartbreaking." Spoiler warning: nobody gets any bad news. . . . In any event, the misnomer is evidence of how little premium our society puts on emotional literacy. Or phrased less pretentiously: being able to name what we're feeling. —George Spyros, "iPhone 4 FaceTime Commercials: Are Apple's TV Ads Really 'Heartbreaking?'" *The Huffington Post*, July 27, 2010

Misnomer also has a specific meaning in law: "an error in name; misstatement in a document of the name of a person." *Misnomers* in proceedings are usually amended by the court, provided no one has been misled or prejudiced by the mistake.

moiety
/ (moi'i-tē)/

noun

1 A half part or share; one of two equal parts: as a moiety of an estate, goods, or profits.

2 A portion; a share.

Examples:

The experts—some scores of them including the British Museum—had affirmed that the drawing was worth a certain moiety of twelve shillings. —Henry Adams, *The Education of Henry Adams*, 1918

The Portuguese Court could raise only a moiety of the dowry, and even that consisted in large part of merchandise and jewels of doubtful value. —Edward Hyde Clarendon and Sir Henry Craik, *Life of Edward Earl of Clarendon*, 1827

To-day, I suppose, if it were possible to indicate, in units of energy, the grand total of work upon which the social fabric of the United States or England rests, it would be found that a vastly preponderating moiety is derived from non-human sources, from coal and liquid fuel, and explosives and wind and water. —H. G. Wells, *A Modern Utopia*, 1936

One half of the world believes the other half to be mad; and who shall decide which moiety is right, the reputed lunatics or the supposed sane, since neither party can be unprejudiced in the matter? —Charles Maurice Davies, *Mystic London: Or Phases of Occult Life in the Metropolis*, 1875

In anthropology, *moiety* refers to "each descent group in a culture that is divided exactly into two descent groups."

75 **nascent**

/ (nas'ənt *or* nā'sənt)/

adjective

• Beginning to exist or to grow; commencing development; coming into being; incipient.

Examples:

Hitherto, since Martha's death, she had found in **nascent**, indolent self-pity the choicest of luxuries. —Amelia Edith Huddleston Barr, *The Measure of a Man*, 1915

Indeed, even those Kindergartens which are professedly exclusive, and which confine their ministrations to the children of one particular neighborhood, are obliged by the nature of things to contain **nascent** individualities of almost every type. —Marion Foster Washburne, *Study of Child Life*, 1907

But now, this large amount of nervous energy, instead of being allowed to expend itself in producing an equivalent amount of the new thoughts and emotions which were **nascent**, is suddenly checked in its flow. —Herbert Spencer, *Essays on Education and Kindred Subjects*, 1911

He said, "Executive coaching is still in **nascent** phase in India, whereas in U.S. and European countries, it is proved to be a powerful tool to improve the quality of leaders." —Sudarshan

Kumar, "Do Indian Leaders Hesitate to Make Independent Decisions?" *Silicon India*, April 20, 2010

The clothes certainly are there—in **nascent** form since the period dealt with here focuses on Chanel's (Audrey Tatou) earlier years. —Dan Persons, "Fashion Defied/Defined: Anne Fontaine on Coco Before Chanel," *The Huffington Post*, September 25, 2009

Nascent comes from the Latin word *nāscī*, meaning "to be born."

nihilism

/ (nī'ə-liz͵əm *or* nē'-ə-liz͵əm)/

noun

1 In metaphysics, the doctrine that nothing can really be known, because nothing exists; the denial of all real existence, and consequently of all knowledge of existences or real things.
2 In theology, same as nihilianism.
3 Total disbelief in religion, morality, law, and order.

Examples:

One straightforward rationale for **nihilism** is the combination of supernaturalism about what makes life meaningful and atheism about whether God exists. If you believe that God or a soul is necessary for meaning in life, and if you believe that neither exists, then you are a nihilist, someone who denies that life has meaning. —"The Meaning of Life," *Stanford Encyclopedia of Philosophy*, May 15, 2007

Legal **nihilism** is at its all-time high, yet the government pretends to believe that all systems are running with regularity. —Robert Amsterdam, "Putin's Big Lie About Khodorkovsky," *The Huffington Post*, December 4, 2009

Cage certainly shares some of their values—these anarchists know how to party, and the women are stunning—but he comes to realize that **nihilism** is less of a kick when innocents die. —"'Xxx' Threat," *Newsweek*, August 5, 2002

Nihilism was originally "a social (not a political) movement in Russia, in opposition to the customary forms of matrimony, the parental authority, and the tyranny of custom." In Latin, *nihil* means "nothing."

77

noisome
/ (noi'səm)/

adjective

1 Hurtful; mischievous; noxious: as a noisome pestilence.
2 Offensive to sight or smell, especially to the latter; producing loathing or disgust; disgusting; specifically, ill-smelling.
3 Disagreeable, in a general sense; extremely offensive.

Examples:

Three years later, after having been imprisoned in noisome cells some thirty times within six years, utterly broken in health, if not weakened also in mind, and never feeling safe from arrest while in his own land, Browne finally sought pardon for his offensive teachings and, obtaining it, reentered the English communion. —M. Louise Greene, *The Development of Religious Liberty in Connecticut*, 1905

The tenement was of rather a superior class. But to Susan it seemed full of noisome smells, and she was offended by the halls littered with evidences of the uncleanness of the tenants. —David Graham Phillips, *Susan Lenox: Her Rise and Fall*, 1917

The fact clearly was that the wretched sewage of Washington, in those days, which was betrayed in all parts of the hotel by every kind of noisome odor, had at last begun to do its work. —Andrew Dickson White, *Autobiography of Andrew Dickson White*, 1906

Noisome contains the Middle English root *noie*, "harm," which is short for the Old French *anoi*, "annoyance."

78 nomenclature
/ (nō'mən-klā͜ˌchər *or* nō-men'klə-ˌchər)/

noun

1 A name.

2 A system of names; the systematic naming of things; specifically, the names of things in any art or science, or the whole vocabulary of names or technical terms that are appropriated to any particular branch of science.

Examples:

So little originality in **nomenclature** is shown in America, that we could desire that Indian names should be retained; that is, when not too long, or harsh in sound; yet in this case we are inclined to rejoice at the change from the aboriginal to the more musical modern title. —Eliza B. Chase, *Over the Border: Acadia, the Home of "Evangeline,"* 1902

Inaccuracy in **nomenclature** is one of the stumbling blocks the student encounters, and the tendency of the day to classify "styles" by the restricted formula of monarchical periods is likewise misleading. —Ada Wentworth Fitzwilliam and A. F. Morris Hands, *Jacobean Embroidery,* 1912

If you're wondering what "Tiguan" means, consider that it's an improvement over Touareg, the name of the company's big, truckish SUV. And before you get too down on the notion of mating a tiger with an iguana, consider that the **nomenclature** is about the cleverest thing VW has done here. —Jeff Sabatini, "Volkswagen's Mini-Me SUV," *The Wall Street Journal*, July 25, 2008

Synonyms for *nomenclature* include *glossary*, *vocabulary*, *terminology*, and *dictionary*.

nonplussed
/ (non-plus'd)/

adjective
• Bewildered; unsure how to respond.

Examples:
Very curtly I asked the gentleman his business. With a surprised, timid manner he faltered that he had met my wife and daughter at Onteora, and they had asked him to call. Fine lie, I thought, and I froze him. He seemed to be kind of **nonplussed**, and sat there fingering the etchings in the case until I told him he needn't bother, because we had those. —Mark Twain, *Mark Twain's Speeches*, 1910

Then again, the first time I met Reagan all he talked about was the money he had saved the taxpayers as governor of California by changing the size of the folders used for storing the state's files. So **nonplussed** was I by the delight he showed at this great achievement that I came close to thinking that my friends were right and that I had made a mistake in supporting him. —Norman Podhoretz, "In Defense of Sarah Palin," *The Wall Street Journal*, March 29, 2010

Maggie was so **nonplussed** by his question that for several seconds she simply stared at him in puzzled silence. —Wordnik

Nonplussed is the adjectival form of *nonplus*, "a state of perplexity; to perplex," which comes from the Latin *non plus*, "no more," meaning one is so confused, nothing more can be said or done.

80   obduracy
/ (ob'door-ə-sē *or* ob'dyoor-ə-sē)/

noun
- The state or quality of being obdurate; especially, the state of being hardened against moral influences; extreme hardness of heart; rebellious persistence in wickedness.

Examples:
The tyrant was moved with her distress; for unfeeling obduracy is the vice only of the old, whose sensibility has been worn away by the habitual perpetration of reiterated wrongs. —John Hawkesworth, *Almoran and Hamet*, 1709

Such a disposition proves that God is inclined to pardon, to endure and to remit the sins of men, if only they will come to their senses; but inasmuch as they continue in **obduracy**, and reject all help, he is, as it were, tormented by this wickedness of men. —Martin Luther, *Commentary on Genesis*, 1910

Even so, events could turn against Republican Machiavellians inasmuch as their **obduracy** is the best thing Democrats have going for them now that Obamamania has all but disappeared. —Andrew Levine, "Republican Machiavellians: Scourge of Democrats—For Tea Partiers, Not So Much," *The Huffington Post*, July 22, 2010

"That he fought to breathe, fought to live, every second of the last 30 years of illness with such mind-blowing **obduracy**, is a testament to the core of who he was," she told mourners. —"'Love Story' Author Erich Segal Dies Aged 72: Family," *The Raw Story*, January 20, 2010

Obduracy comes from the Latin word *obdūrāre*, meaning "to harden."

81

obstreperous
/ (ob-strep′ər-əs *or* əb-strep′ər-əs)/

adjective
• Making a great noise or outcry.

Examples:

This fanatico of mine, walking home from the theater one night with two other like-minded individuals, indulged himself in **obstreperous** abuse of poor Mr. Abbot, in which he was heartily joined by his companions. —Fanny Kemble, *Records of a Girlhood*, 1880

And soon as it come to me, why, I jest named the **obstreperous** one Hope and the quiet one Faith—don't you see? —Fannie E. Newberry, *All Aboard, A Story for Girls*, 1898

Meanwhile, the royal cachinnation was echoed out by a discordant and portentous laugh from behind the arras, like that of one who, little accustomed to give way to such emotions, feels himself at some particular impulse unable either to control or to modify his **obstreperous** mirth. —Sir Walter Scott, *The Fortunes of Nigel*, 1822

We climbed a bit, then a bit more trying to find our friend the tailwind, but she was gone. She'd been replaced by her adversary, a big **obstreperous** huffing puffing sky filling monster with but one goal—to get us WET! —Sam Isaac Edwards, "Cuba: Five Days on the Cheap, Free Cell, Free Guard Dog, Free Guard," *The Huffington Post*, March 29, 2010

Synonyms for *obstreperous* include *clamorous, vociferous, noisy, boisterous, tumultuous, uproarious,* and *unruly.*

82 **omertà**

/ (ō-mûr'tə *or* ō͝mer-tä')/

noun

- A code of silence among members of a criminal organization (especially the Mafia) that forbids divulging insider secrets to law enforcement.

Examples:

[Sopranos creator David] Chase is so paranoid about leaking plot points, it's as if he's forced everyone connected with the show to take an oath of **omertà**. —Peter Biskind, "An American Family," *Vanity Fair*, April 2007

Before Al Franken took his oath of "Don't Ask, Don't Tell" and sat quietly at his desk in the Senate chamber, where decorum is enforced like **omertà**, he published a book about George W. Bush titled *Lies (And the Lying Liars Who Tell Them)*. —David Colbert, "Political Celebrity and Publishing Tastes," *The Huffington Post*, October 6, 2009

Old Man Lubitsch is singing to her in the language of the old country, and his shadowed, sharp little eyes lay **omertà** upon me, dark and deep; these are secrets between men, boy, between the true men of the heart. —Nick Harkaway, "Book Excerpt: The Gone-Away World," *The Wall Street Journal*, August 29, 2008

Omertà is Italian in origin and is perhaps an alteration of the word *umiltà*, meaning "humility, modesty," which comes from the Latin *humilitās*.

83   opprobrium
/ (ə-prō'brē-əm)/

noun
- Imputation of shameful conduct; insulting reproach; contumely; scurrility.

Examples:

The language of insults and **opprobrium** is particularly rich in such double meanings. The pig god, wishing to insult Pélé, who has refused his advances, sings of her, innocently enough to common ears, as a "woman pounding *noni*." Now, the noni is the plant from which red dye is extracted; the allusion therefore is to Pélé's red eyes, and the goddess promptly resents the implication. —Martha Warren Beckwith, *The Hawaiian Romance of Laieikawai*, 1917

The appellation, which was bestowed upon them in **opprobrium**, and which they certainly wore in no meek manner, but evidently gloried in as a word of highest praise and honor, I use as a convenient one to characterize the idea I would represent. —"Southern Hate of New England," *Continental Monthly*, September 1863

When this kind of **opprobrium** is peddled by major media outlets, it's high time that the Democratic establishment and the larger progressive community understand that this is a make-or-break showdown with the media. —Peter Daou, "Ann Coulter Identifies John Murtha as a Target for Murder," *The Huffington Post*, June 15, 2006

Synonyms for *opprobrium* include *obloquy, infamy, ignominy, odium, disgrace, reproach, contempt,* and *dishonor.*

(84) otiose
/ (ō'tē-ōs)/

adjective

1 Being at rest or ease; not at work; unemployed; inactive; idle.

2 Made, done, or performed in a leisurely, half-hearted way; perfunctory, negligent; careless; ineffective; vain; futile; to no purpose.

Examples:

And these examples, given due and detailed attention, will exhibit a context-sensitive particularity that makes generalized pronouncements hovering high above the ground of that detail look **otiose**, inattentive, or, more bluntly, just a plain falsification of experience. —"Wittgenstein's Aesthetics," *Stanford Encyclopedia of Philosophy*, January 26, 2007

Vanity Fair has now quite transcended the café society of its earlier incarnation. On one night of the year, it dominates Hollywood with an enviable reception. On another, it has the whole attention of the Cannes Film Festival with what it would be **otiose** to call a hot ticket. —Christopher Hitchens, "The V.F. Century," *Vanity Fair*, October 2008

There is the polite, if **otiose**, query as to whether one has finished eating. There follows the equally **otiose** inquiry if one was alone or not. —Iftekhar Sayeed, "Food," OpEdNews.com, March 3, 2009

The sooner we quit fiddling with **otiose** sanctions against Iran, the sooner we can begin crafting containment and deterrence strategies that are actually effective. —Michael Hughes, "Who Cares If Iran Goes Nuclear?" *The Huffington Post*, April 25, 2010

Otiose is from the Latin word *ōtiōsus,* meaning "idle."

85 **overhaul**
/ (ō͵vər-hôl' *or* ō'vər-hôl͵)/

verb

1 To turn over for examination; examine thoroughly with a view to repairs.

2 To reexamine, as accounts.

3 To gain upon; make up with; overtake.
4 To search a ship for contraband goods.

noun
• Examination; inspection; repair.

Examples:
The failings of the system have stirred significant discontent, and the overhaul is a response to those social pressures.
—Gordon Fairclough, "Beijing Plans $124 Billion Overhaul of Health Care," *The Wall Street Journal*, January 22, 2009

Substitute sex for money and you have what the folks over at Change Congress are pushing: that donors go "on strike," refusing to give their money to pols until a campaign finance overhaul is passed (specifically, they favor a system whereby people limiting themselves to small donations would get matching government funds). —Lawrence Lessig, "Change Congress—We're Bringing Sexy Back," *The Huffington Post*, January 27, 2009

Their main objection: If a central goal of regulatory overhaul is to make financial markets more transparent and accountable, Lincoln's provision would have the opposite effect. —Brady Dennis, "Derivatives-Spinoff Proposal Opposed as Part of Overhaul Bill," *The Washington Post*, May 4, 2010

Overhaul was formed by combining *over* and *haul,* which comes from the Middle English *haulen,* "to pull in fishing nets."

86

parvenu
/ (pär'və-nōō, *or* pär'və-nyōō,)/

noun

- One newly risen into notice, especially by an accident of fortune and beyond his or her birth or apparent deserts, whether as a claimant for a place in society or as occupying a position of authority; an upstart.

Examples:

It is true they made their morning calls, and invited the former Viscountess de Beauharnais, with her daughter, to their evening receptions; but they carefully avoided being present at the evening circles of Madame Bonaparte, where their exclusiveness was beset with the danger of coming in contact with some "parvenu," or with some sprig of the army, or of the financial bureaus. —L. Mühlbach, *Empress Josephine,* 1910

Waizero Terunish was proud; she always looked on her husband as a "parvenu," and took no pains to hide from him her want of respect and affection. —Dr. Henri Blanc, *Narrative of Captivity in Abyssinia,* 1868

The house had been purchased during the Terror by the father of Mlle. Gamard, a dealer in wood, a kind of **parvenu** peasant. —Anatole Cerfberr and Jules Francois Christophe, *Repertory of the Comedie Humaine*, 1843

Not content with such a spectacular windfall, the caddish Chan—the kind of **parvenu**, incidentally, who names his eldest son Wealthee—considers himself entitled the rest of her estate, even though he would be depriving a charity of its use, should he win control of it. —Liam Fitzpatrick, "How Feng Shui Is Being Discredited in Hong Kong," *Time*, December 21, 2009

Parvenu is from the French word *parvenir*, meaning "to arrive."

peripatetic

/ (per͵ə-pə-tet'ik)/

adjective

1 Walking about; itinerant.

2 When capitalized, *Peripatetic* means about or pertaining to Aristotle's system of philosophy, or the sect of his followers; Aristotelian: as the *Peripatetic* philosophers.

Examples:

That afternoon we were on the march in what Denham called our **peripatetic** hospital; but he was not happy. — George Manville Fenn, *Charge! A Story of Briton and Beer*, 1890

111

The current gotta-have-it among the wired **peripatetic** is an ultralight, laptop-computer-size satellite terminal with an antenna built into the lid—which will set you back $1,500. —"Googling at 5,000 Meters," *Newsweek*, June 7, 2004

After traveling the globe for years, Alex finally decided to give up the **peripatetic** lifestyle of a photojournalist and settle in his hometown to sell portraits of pets. —Wordnik

Cleverly staged by Christopher Haydon, with a **peripatetic** audience, it's also a model of how spectators can be made to keep moving—in this case by the genially cajoling Bragg— around a building and through a plot. —Susannah Clapp, "1000 Revolutions per Moment; Pressure Drop," *The Guardian*, May 2, 2010

Peripatetic comes from the Greek word *peripatein*, "to walk about," or *peripatos*, "covered walk," which is supposedly where Aristotle lectured.

88 peruse
/ (pə-rōōz') /

verb

1 To go through searchingly or carefully; run over with careful scrutiny; examine throughout or in detail; inspect; survey; scan; scrutinize.

2 To read through carefully or with attention.

Examples:

On the 22nd June the Chamberlain was instructed to prepare with all convenient speed four dozen good splentes and as many good sallettes or sculles for the city's use, and to cause a bowyer to "**peruse**" the city's bows and to put them in such good order that they might be serviceable when required. —Reginald R. Sharpe, *London and the Kingdom*, 1894

We had had dozens of furnishing lists to **peruse** from the principal houses in London and Paris, as if even there it was a well-understood thing that Julia and I were going to be married. —Hesba Stretton, *The Doctor's Dilemma*, 1872

What this month's release schedule lacks in overall Sound-Scan-measured sales impact, it more than makes up for in music-geek esteem: the National, Broken Social Scene, LCD Soundsystem, the New Pornographers, and the Hold Steady are all familiar entities to those who **peruse** critics' year-end "best of" ballots. —Seth Colter Walls, "May: Indie Rock's Month of the Year!" *Newsweek*, May 5, 2010

Peruse is from the Middle English word *perusen,* meaning "to use up."

89 picaresque

/ (pik̩ə-resk' *or* pē̩kə-resk')/

adjective

- Pertaining to or dealing with rogues: used of literary productions that deal with the fortunes of rogues or adventurers.

Examples:

They belonged mostly to that class of realistic fiction which is called **picaresque**, from the Spanish word "picaro," a rogue, because it began in Spain with the "Lazarillo de Tormes" of Diego de Mendoza, in 1553, and because its heroes are knavish serving-boys or similar characters whose unprincipled tricks and exploits formed the substance of the stories. —Robert Huntington Fletcher, *A History of English Literature*, 1919

[Robert Louis] Stevenson and [Rudyard] Kipling have proved its immense popularity, with the whole brood of detective stories and the tales of successful rascality we call "**picaresque**." —Charlotte Perkins Gilman, *Our Androcentric Culture*, 1911

The Wife of Bath is always brought up at this point as the mother of the **picaresque** heroine (although today she'd be said to have anger management issues), as well as her modern-day heir, before Gilbert, the heroine of Erica Jong's

Fear of Flying. —Emma Brockes, "Eat, Pray, Cash In," *The Guardian*,
August 14, 2010

Picaresque is from the Spanish word *picaro*, meaning "rogue, thief,
or pirate," and should not be confused with *picturesque*, "picture-like;
strikingly graphic or vivid."

picayune
/ (pik͜ə-yo͞on')/

adjective

1 Petty, trivial; of little consequence; small and of little importance; picayunish.

2 Small-minded: being childishly spiteful, tending to go on
about unimportant things.

noun

1 Something not worth arguing about.

2 An argument, fact, corner case, or other issue raised
(often intentionally) that distracts from a larger issue at
hand or does not change a primary supposition, outcome,
postulate, premise, conclusion, hypothesis, judgment, or
recommendation.

3 A small coin of the value of six and a quarter cents. A
5-cent or 6-cent piece.

Examples:

It seems kind of **picayune** in the grand context of the stimulus effort. —Robert O'Harrow Jr., "Government Inc.," *The Washington Post*, June 17, 2009

Some chefs and owners at the city's elite restaurants expressed horror at the idea that what they called **picayune** infractions would be lumped together with problems at the corner greasy spoon. —Thomas J. Lueck and Niel Macfarquhar, "Site Listing Restaurant Inspections Starts a Feeding Frenzy on the Web," *The New York Times*, May 18, 2000

But this is the Magic-Eye effect of the reality genre: It confuses public and private concerns, magnifies the **picayune** and annihilates perspective. —Scott Brown, "Mark Sanford: Reality Television Superstar," *The Huffington Post*, July 2, 2009

Picayune is from the Louisiana French word *picaillon,* meaning "small coin," and was formerly the Spanish half-real, equal to 1 and 1/6 of a dollar, or 6¼ cents.

(91) **plethora**

/ (pleth'ər-ə)/

noun

- Overfullness in any respect; superabundance.

Examples:

Such redoubtables as Red Dog, Little Big Man, Prowling Wolf, and Kills Asleep were swaggering about, as were their young men, in **plethora** of savage adornment and "store clothes." —Charles King, *Under Fire*, 1895

The remedy for your **plethora** is simple—abstinence. —Thomas Moore, *Life of Lord Byron*, 1835

This, no doubt, explains my unfamiliarity with the name of Miss Katharine Newlin Burt, also certain minor points, notably the fact that the story, though by no means badly told, suffers from what I can only call a **plethora** of plot. —"Our Booking Office," *Punch or the London Charivari*, March 24, 1920

And the curious effect of this "mot d'ordre" was that the pursuit arrested the attention as the most essential, and the happiness was postponed, almost invariably, to some future season, when leisure or **plethora**, that is, relaxation or gorged desire, should induce that physical and moral glow which is commonly accepted as happiness. —Charles Dudley Warner, *Nine Short Essays*, late 1800s

She said she received a "**plethora**" of e-mails from residents who raised concerns that she agreed with. —Nathan Pipenberg, "Council Requests Public Hearings," *The Daily Collegian*, April 6, 2010

117

Synonyms for *plethora* include *excess, glut, overfullness, repletion, slew, overabundance,* and *superabundance.* In pathology, *plethora* is also known as *hyperemia,* as opposed to *anemia,* "a deficiency of blood in a living body."

92 prelapsarian
/ (prē͵lap-sâr'ē-ən)/

adjective

1 Of, or relating to the period before the fall of Adam and Eve.

2 Characteristic of or pertaining to any carefree or innocent period.

Examples:

For a generation raised on divorce, the Trillins—who married in 1965, just before the marriage-hopping baby boomers came of age—represent a kind of **prelapsarian** parental ideal. —Lizzy Ratner, "Calvin Trillin Loves His Wife," *The New York Observer,* January 14, 2007

The danger in writing about the **prelapsarian** period of the late 1990s—just before all the calamities started to strike—is false nostalgia: false because all the signs of imminent decline and collapse were there already. —Anis Shivani, "The Best Post-9/11 Novel: Huffington Post Interviews Teddy Wayne, Author of 'Kapitoil,'" *The Huffington Post,* June 7, 2010

Bosch's large and elaborate triptych attracts the bigger crowds, and it's easy to see why. His naked men and women and fantastic animals can be viewed as drug-addled comedy. . . . Even scholars can't agree if the arcane allegory is a remonstration about the demons of lust or the dream of a **prelapsarian** paradise before sex became sinful. —Richard B. Woodward, "Death Takes No Holiday," *The Wall Street Journal*, February 14, 2009

Prelapsarian is made up of the Latin *pre*, "before," and *lāpsus*, "fall."

(93) prescient
/ (presh'ənt, presh'-ē-ənt, prē'shənt, *or* prē'-shē-ənt)/

adjective
• Foreknowing; having knowledge of events before they take place.

Examples:
Public know-it-alls are on display 24/7 in what media maven Ken Auletta calls the "endless argument" —talk radio/cable news/blogosphere. Take the oleaginous Dick Morris, who's wrong so often you're better off believing the opposite of what he says. (Recall his **prescient** volume "Condi vs. Hillary," published before the 2008 Presidential election campaign.) —Michael Sigman, "Knowing Know-It-Alls," *The Huffington Post*, January 25, 2010

It will make rental royalty out of those **prescient** people who moved into illegal lofts in the former frontier and now-chic neighborhoods. —Cara Buckley, "That Cheap, Roomy Sunny Loft Can Now Be a Legal One, Too," *The New York Times*, July 26, 2010

Joniec also recalled a **prescient** line he had penned in a letter to his girlfriend, Anne Sysol, just months before: "We expect to be in action soon, that being with Japan." —Art Carey, "A Day That Will Live in Infamy Is a Day Many Will Never Forget," *Rutland Herald*, December 6, 2009

Synonyms for *prescient* include *foreseeing, foreknowing, clairvoyant, precognizant,* and *previsive.*

94

profligate

/ (prof'li-git *or* prof'li-gāt,)/

adjective

1 Overthrown; conquered; defeated.

2 Ruined in morals; abandoned to vice; lost to principle, virtue, or decency; extremely vicious; shamelessly wicked.

noun

• An abandoned person; one who has lost all regard for good principles, virtue, or decency.

Examples:

What if a new government repudiates these promises and engages in **profligate** ways? Taxpayers in states contributing to the bailout might as well kiss their money goodbye. —Sandeep Gopalan, "A Hybrid Conservatorship Model for Greece?" *The Huffington Post*, March 25, 2010

For, as well as I can guess, if that **profligate** is in favour with our tyrants, he will be able to crow not only over the "cynic consular," but over your Tritons of the fish-ponds also. —*The Letters of Cicero*, 1899

Now, the **profligate** is he who wishes to spread this crimson of conscious joy over everything; to have excitement at every moment; to paint everything red. He bursts a thousand barrels of wine to incarnadine the streets; and sometimes (in his last madness) he will butcher beasts and men to dip his gigantic brushes in their blood. —G. K. Chesterton, *Alarms and Discursions*, 1910

Profligate comes from the Latin word *prōflīgāre*, meaning "to ruin, cast down."

95 **propinquity**
/ (prə-ping'kwi-tē)/

noun

1 Nearness in place; neighborhood.
2 Nearness in time.
3 Nearness of blood; kindred.

Examples:

Juxtaposition—or you may call it **propinquity**—or, if you like, being rather too near for one maintaining the position of an ideal. —O. Henry, *The Four Million*, 1906

But the Baroness believed much in **propinquity**; and she brought the rector and Alice together as often as possible, and coached the girl in coquettish arts when alone with her, and credited her with witticisms and bon-mots which she had never uttered, when talking of her to the young rector. —Ella Wheeler Wilcox, *An Ambitious Man*, 1896

The only reason Joanne stayed in touch with the irritating girl was **propinquity**—they were cousins, their mothers sisters. —Wordnik

Synonyms for *propinquity* include *proximity, affiliation, kindred, neighborhood, vicinity, closeness, juxtaposition,* and *adjacency.*

96   **provenance**

/ (prov'ə-nəns *or* prov'ə-näns͵)/

noun

- Origin; source or quarter from which anything comes; provenience: especially in the sense of "place of manufacture, production, or discovery."

Examples:

Most dependable dealers and auction houses will stand by their wares—forever. That, plus credible provenance, is pretty good insurance if you're laying down $50,000 for a book. —Tom Post, "Moses Signed My Bible," *Forbes*, December 10, 2009

At the close of my original article, I quoted my wife—whose tribal provenance is none of your business—as saying that "women get funnier as they get older." —Christopher Hitchens, "Why Women Still Don't Get It," *Vanity Fair*, March 3, 2008

Thus, after an exhaustive and occasionally exhausting tour of North American oysters—most are from one of two species, Eastern or Pacific, but regional provenance is as important as species, since flavor and texture are influenced by temperature, currents and salinity—Mr. Jacobsen gets practical. —Aram Bakshian Jr., "Gastronomy," *The Wall Street Journal*, October 20, 2007

The meaning of *provenance* changes slightly depending on context. In archaeology, *provenance* is "the place and time of origin of some artifact"; in art, "the history of ownership of a work of art." When used of a person, it means "background, ancestry."

97

pusillanimous
/ (pyō͞o͝sə-lan'ə-məs)/

adjective

1 Lacking strength and firmness of mind; wanting in courage and fortitude; being of weak courage; faint-hearted; mean-spirited; cowardly.

2 Proceeding from lack of courage; indicating timidity.

Examples:

"How childish you are, Eva!" said the one, "with your fears and your doubts! and how **pusillanimous** is your love. If you would learn, lovely angel! how true love speaks, listen to me." —Fredrika Bremer, *The Home*, 1853

The bipartisan failure to prevent North Korea from becoming a nuclear weapons state, and the almost certain failure of this administration and other **pusillanimous** states to prevent Iran from soon joining that group, lead me to wonder about the wisdom of agreeing to further reductions in our nuclear forces when such a commitment limits us, no matter what other nations aside from Russia may do. —Lawrence S.

Eagleburger, "It Is Important to Get Nuclear Weapons Policy Right," *The Wall Street Journal*, July 15, 2009

We have been laborious, contented, and prosperous; and if we have been reabsorbed by the mother country, in accordance with what I cannot but call the **pusillanimous** conduct of certain of our elder Britannulists, it has not been from any failure on the part of the island, but from the opposition with which the Fixed Period has been regarded. — Anthony Trollope, *The Fixed Period*, 1882

Pusillanimous comes from the Latin word *pusillus,* meaning "weak," which is a diminutive of *pullus,* meaning "the young of an animal."

98 **putative**
/ (pyōō′tə-tiv)/

adjective
• Supposed; reputed; commonly thought or deemed: as the putative father of a child.

Examples:
As a result, whatever **putative** solutions were agreed upon will remain **putative**; and, even if the Pakistani army makes temporary headway against the Taliban in Swat and elsewhere, the problem will continue to fester and undermine the viability of Pakistan and Afghanistan alike. —Alex Alexiev,

"Washington's Misguided Pakistan Policy," *National Review Online*, May 7, 2009

Perhaps the specter of losing the nomination after being dubbed the **putative** front runner, or of gaining the nomination in a bitterly divisive nomination contest then losing the presidency, might be likened to a Pyrrhic victory. —Gloria Feldt, "Which Greek Tragedy Are Bill and Hillary Enacting?" *The Huffington Post*, January 28, 2008

Many Obama administration officials are also skeptical of reopening the so-called six-party talks with North Korea, which also involve China, Japan, Russia and South Korea. Instead, the administration is trying to persuade China to take a stronger line with North Korea, a **putative** ally that is deeply dependent on China. —Yochi J. Dreazen, "U.S. Fortifies Hawaii to Meet Threat from Korea," *The Wall Street Journal*, June 19, 2009

Putative comes from the Latin word *putāre*, meaning "to think."

quixotic
/ (kwik-sot'ik)/

adjective

• Extravagantly or absurdly romantic; striving for an unattainable or impracticable ideal; characterized by futile self-devotion; visionary.

126

Examples:

Billionaires tend to engage in quixotic legacy-building, and if we buy the thrust of David Kirkpatrick's crisply written "The Facebook Effect," Facebook was imbued with a certain purity from the beginning. —David Harsanyi, "David Kirkpatrick's 'The Facebook Effect,'" *The Washington Post*, June 27, 2010

Only his ears kept it from dragging him to earth and smothering him, and now as he looked up at the sky I saw clear cut against its blackness a thin quixotic visage, shaded by a growth of stubble beard. —Nelson Lloyd, *David Malcolm*, 1913

Affirmation-starved France usually loves global titles of any kind (one big reason why French competitors tend to out-number foreign rivals in quixotic contests like reverse round-the-world solo yachting races and France's annual international plum-spitting tournaments). —Bruce Crumley, "French Tourists: Still the World's Worst," *Time*, July 10, 2009

Now that he knew where she was he made no attempt to visit her,—he was too grieved and disappointed at her continued absence, and deeply hurt at what he considered her "quixotic" conduct in adopting a different name,—an "alias" as he called it. —Marie Corelli, Innocent, *Her Fancy and His Fact*, 1914

Quixotic comes from Don Quixote, the hero of Miguel Cervantes's celebrated novel. The full title is *The Ingenious Hidalgo Don Quixote of La Mancha.*

100 **quotidian**
/ (kwō-tid'ē-ən)/

adjective
• Daily; occurring or returning daily.

noun
• Something that returns or is expected every day; specifically, in medicine, a fever whose paroxysms return every day.

Examples:

Life in Afghanistan had been so bleak that **quotidian** things like girls attending school, women leaving their homes, people dancing, and children flying kites were hailed as extraordinary events. —Katherine Brown, "Afghanistan's Other Time Warp," *The Huffington Post*, July 3, 2010

Eschewing literary subjects for motifs that were purely visual, Renoir also began to paint half-length views of solitary women engaged in **quotidian** pursuits, and a long wall is devoted to these intimate, tranquil canvases. —Mary Tompkins

Lewis, "Impressions of an Aging Artist," *The Wall Street Journal*, March 24, 2010

The new edition has finally cottoned on to social media and microblogging. Slightly less **quotidian** is the phrase dictionary attack, which describes an attempt to gain illicit access to a computer system by using an enormous set of words to generate potential passwords. —Sam Jones, "Climate Change and the Vuvuzela Leave Mark on Oxford Dictionary of English," *The Guardian*, August 19, 2010

In medicine, a *quotidian* fever returns every day and may stem from a chronic illness such as malaria.

101 recondite
/ (rek'ən-dīt, *or* ri-kon'dīt,)/

adjective
1 Hidden from mental view; secret; abstruse: as recondite causes of things.
2 Profound; dealing with things abstruse.

Examples:
Aylmer had converted those smoky, dingy, sombre rooms, where he had spent his brightest years in **recondite** pursuits, into a series of beautiful apartments not unfit to be

the secluded abode of a lovely woman. —Nathaniel Hawthorne, "The Birthmark," *The Short-Story*, 1916

We knew that he was engaged in recondite researches of a scientific nature, and that he possessed a private laboratory, although none of us had ever entered it. —Garrett Putman Serviss, *A Columbus of Space*, 1911

To him, a perfectly unintelligible will is a thing of beauty and a joy for ever; especially if associated with some kind of recondite knavery. —R. Austin Freeman, *The Eye of Osiris*, 1911

"[*Grey Gardens*] was one of the films that all of us quoted to each other," Rhodes says. "It served as a kind of recondite, East Village version of camp, classical Hollywood." —David Colman, "The Cult of Grey Gardens," *The Advocate*, April 2009

In entomology, or the study of insects, *recondite* refers to "organs that are concealed in repose," such as a stinger, as opposed to those that are *exserted*, "protruded."

102 redoubtable
/ (ri-dou'tə-bəl)/

adjective
1 That is to be dreaded; formidable; terrible.
2 Worthy of reverence.

Examples:

Lucien watched this Dauriat, who addressed Finot with the familiar *tu*, which even Finot did not permit himself to use in reply; who called the redoubtable Blondet "my boy," and extended a hand royally to Nathan with a friendly nod. — Honoré de Balzac, A *Distinguished Provincial at Paris*, 1901

But, Charles having got over to Scotland where the men of the Solemn League and Covenant led him a prodigiously dull life and made him very weary with long sermons and grim Sundays, the Parliament called the redoubtable Oliver home to knock the Scottish men on the head for setting up that Prince. —Charles Dickens, A *Child's History of England*, 1876

The coalition cabinet has only four female members: Caroline Spelman at environment, Cheryl Gillan, the Welsh secretary, Tory party chairman Baroness Warsi and the redoubtable May herself, who seems to be able to get away with being forthright on women's issues without attracting the vilification heaped on Harriet Harman, if only because she has entranced male commentators with her kitten heels. —Ruth Sunderland, "This Austerity Budget Acts as a Woman-Seeking Missile," *The Guardian*, August 8, 2010

The *redoubtable* hero is often seen in irony or burlesque, a kind of dramatic extravaganza usually based on a serious play or subject, with music.

131

103 **renascent**
/ (ri-nas'ənt *or* ri-nā'sənt)/

adjective
- Springing or rising into being again; reproduced; reappearing; rejuvenated.

Examples:

Despite many centuries of relative neglect, the old traditions lived on, cherished by scholars, until now, at the beginning of the twentieth century, the Icelandic mind appears to be again **renascent** and creative. —Jóhann Sigurjónsson, *Modern Icelandic Plays*, 1916

For our drama is **renascent**, and nothing will stop its growth. It is not **renascent** because this or that man is writing, but because of a new spirit. —John Galsworthy, *The Inn of Tranquility, Studies and Essays*, 1913

Tapping the frustration of protesters—including a **renascent** and mainstreamed "tea bag" movement—the former captains and sergeants, the ex-CIA operatives and out-of-work private mercenaries of the War on Terror take action. —William Astore, "A Very American Coup: Coming Soon to a Hometown Near You," *The Huffington Post*, January 19, 2010

Mr. Obama far outdistances Mr. Clinton, however, in telling the story of America in a way that reinforces a **renascent** liberalism. —Charles R. Kesler, "The Audacity of Barack Obama," *The Wall Street Journal*, October 21, 2008

Renascent comes from the Latin word *renāscī*, meaning "to be born again," and is related to *renaissance*, "a rebirth or revival."

(104) **reticent**
/ (retˈi-sənt)/

adjective
- Disposed to be silent; reserved; not apt to speak about or reveal any matters.

Examples:
A mind so capacious and so **reticent** is always an enigma to near observers. —"Reviews and Literary Notices," *The Atlantic Monthly*, November 1862

In this regard, the monitors have noted that the supporters of many returning politicians remain **reticent** and fearful of the future and that there is minimal activity in the provinces by those parties in opposition to those in the Royal Government. —"United Nations: Report of the Special Representative of the Secretary-General on the Situation of Human Rights in Cambodia," *Cambodia*, 1998

With its Asian researchers struggling, P&G executives began experimenting in 2006 with a program intended to help Asian researchers develop the confidence to speak their minds . . . Procter veterans attempt to retrain **reticent** employees and help them learn to thrive in the outwardly challenging environment at P&G. —Roger O. Crockett, "P&G Gets Reticent Researchers to Speak Up," *Bloomberg Businessweek*, October 2, 2009

Molly's eyes were watery and her nose red, but she remained **reticent** as to what might be wrong. —Wordnik

Reticent comes from the Latin word *reticēre*, meaning "to keep silent," which contains the word *tacēre*, meaning "to be silent," and is related to *taciturn*, "silent or reserved in speech."

salacious
/ (sə-lā'shəs)/

adjective
• Lustful; lecherous.

Examples:
In this one hour, weekly, CBS procedural, Alicia Florrick, who Julianna Margulies adroitly portrays, must pick up their pieces when Peter Florrick, her attorney general husband is caught in **salacious** sex and corruption scandals and lands in

prison. —Catie Lazarus, "The Good Wife Goes to Better Heights," *The Huffington Post*, October 21, 2009

That the content their platforms serve ranges from flirtatious to **salacious** is almost an aside, except for the intensity with which these sex-tech entrepreneurs discuss age-verification options and content restrictions enforced by the wireless carriers. —Regina Lynn, "All Business, No Boobies," *Wired*, October 13, 20

She crossed the street to avoid the bar where drunk and **salacious** men loitered around the doorway, eyeballing and catcalling every woman who walked by. —Wordnik

Salacious comes from the Latin word *salax*, meaning "fond of leaping, lustful," after the idea of male animals leaping on females when mating.

sanguine
/ (san'gwin)/

adjective
1 Bloodthirsty; bloody.
2 Of the color of blood; red; ruddy.
3 Characterized by vitality, vivacious; cheerful; hopeful; confident; ardent; hopefully inclined.

Examples:

His sleep appears untroubled; and, notwithstanding all the terrors of the last few days, I entertain **sanguine** hopes of his immediate recovery. —Paul Adrien, *Willis the Pilot*, 1875

The **sanguine** is known by a stout, well-defined form, a full face, florid complexion, moderate plumpness, firm flesh, chestnut or sandy hair, and blue eyes. This is the tough, hardy, working temperament, excessively fond of exercise and activity, and a great aversion to muscular quiescence and inactivity, and consequently averse to books and close literary pursuits. —Anonymous, *The Ladies' Book of Useful Information*, 1896

For the moment, most analysts remain **sanguine** about BP's ability to weather the storm; 34 of them have "buy" recommendations on the stock, eight have "hold" and only one has a "sell." —Guy Chazan and Neil King Jr., "BP Faces Bleaker Prospects If 'Top Kill' Fails to Stanch Spill," *The Wall Street Journal*, May 25, 2010

Synonyms for *sanguine* include *vivacious, hopeful, confident, ardent, adventurous, buoyant, cheerful, credulous, enthusiastic, excitable,* and *fearless*.

136

(107) schadenfreude
/ (shäd'n-froi͟͟,də)/

noun

- Malicious enjoyment derived from observing someone else's misfortune.

Examples:

[Schadenfreude] means taking pleasure in someone else's misfortune. Now, if you're an average Joe and something bad happens, well, people usually feel sympathy for you. But let's say you're a big, important politician and you've made a lot of enemies. If you take a big fall, all those enemies are going to be mighty happy. And that is **schadenfreude**. —"Eliot Spitzer Resigns," CNN Transcripts, March 12, 2008

In this tsunami of self-celebration, self-promoting moguls need to understand this: We're not happy for you. . . . The millions of the rest of us want to be you, sue you, or prosecute you. We associate outrageous lifestyles with malfeasance, perhaps to justify our own workaday existences, and we revel in **schadenfreude**—we want to enjoy your misfortune. —Eric Dezenhall, "Resentment and Consequences in the New Gilded Age," *The Huffington Post*, June 8, 2007

It means lines that snake through endless hallways so everyone can pack into the pre-conference keynote to watch

Microsoft's Bill Gates squirm uncomfortably as Conan O'Brien pokes fun at him (it didn't help that several Microsoft demos didn't work correctly, eliciting a certain giggly schadenfreude from the audience). —Michael Grebb, "CES Celebrates Gadget Gluttony," *Wired*, January 7, 2005

Schadenfreude comes from the German words *Schaden*, "damage," and *Freude*, "joy."

sclerotic
/ (sklə-rot′ik)/

adjective
• Hard and insular, as in sclerotic bureaucracy.

Examples:
The French Alps offered a holiday weekend from hell just days before Christmas. For 24 miserable hours, cars backed up—and piled up—in sclerotic masses clogging the narrow mountain valleys. —Christopher Dickey, "Remodeling the Slopes," *Newsweek*, January 6, 1992

When Robert Templer wrote *Shadows and Wind* in the late 1990s, Vietnam was a sclerotic country mired in economic crisis and unwilling to make the changes necessary to unleash its innate dynamism. —Bill Hayton, "Vietnam, Rising Dragon," *The Wall Street Journal*, April 1, 2010

Having come from a large and **sclerotic** corporation where change was not only difficult but positively discouraged, Sam had to adjust to his small and innovative new workplace. —Wordnik

Literally, *sclerotic* refers to "the abnormal hardening of body tissues, such as an artery."

109 **sessile**
/ (ses'īl, *or* ses'əl)/

adjective

1 Permanently attached to a substrate; not free to move about; as a sessile oyster.

2 Attached directly by the base; not having an intervening stalk; as a sessile leaf.

Examples:

The blossom, we see, consists of several small spikelets; there are eighteen on our stem. They grow alternately on two opposite sides of the stem, first one on one side, then one on the other. They have no stalk of their own; they are sessile or seated on the stem. —Arthur Owens Cooke, *Wildflowers of the Farm*, 1913

Many ponds are seasonal, lasting just a couple of months (such as sessile pools) while lakes may exist for hundreds

of years or more. —"Freshwater Biomes," *The Encyclopedia of Earth,*
April 1, 2007

A cock yellowhammer sings insistently from a laburnum
tree as I quit the lanes and walk woodland paths where
last anemones wilt into emerald moss. Dappling shafts of
sun turn bluebells to a low running flame, hyacinth scent
pooling in still air. Holly brakes, tangles of rowan and birch,
and **sessile** oak saplings, all witness the seethe of spring and
battle for light. —Jim Perrin, "Country Diary: Harlech," *The Guardian,*
May 29, 2010

Sessile comes from the Latin word *sessilis,* meaning "low, sitting."

shibboleth
/ (shib'ə-lith *or* shib'ə-leth͵)/

noun

1 A word, especially seen as a test, to distinguish someone
as belonging to a particular nation, class, profession, etc.
2 A common or longstanding belief, custom, or catch-
phrase associated with a particular group, especially one
with little current meaning or truth.

Examples:
Some of them—rare and strange souls even in their time—
would have known what they meant and meant what they

said in a way they had as yet only the power to express through the medium of a certain shibboleth, the rest would have used the same forms merely because shibboleth is easy and always safe and creditable. —Frances Hodgson Burnett, *The Head of the House of Coombe*, 1922

A shibboleth is generally defined as a peculiarity of pronunciation or language usage distinguishing an insider from and outsider. For example, back in the late 1960s and early 70s, television characters over the age of twenty-five would say, "I'm hep" instead of "I'm hip," thereby revealing themselves to be "squares." —Jeff Dorchen, "Shibbolethism," *The Huffington Post*, May 4, 2007

Shibboleth is a Hebrew word meaning "ear of corn; stream" and was used to distinguish one tribe that pronounced the word with a *sh* sound from another that pronounced it with an *s* sound.

solecism
/ (sol'i-siz͟ əm *or* sō'li-siz͟ əm)/

noun
1 A gross deviation from the settled usages of grammar; a gross grammatical error, such as "I *done* it" for "I *did* it."
2 Loosely, any small blunder in speech.
3 Any unfitness, absurdity, or impropriety, as in behavior; a violation of the conventional rules of society.

4 An incongruity; an inconsistency; that which is incongruous with the nature of things or with its surroundings; an unnatural phenomenon or product; a prodigy; a monster.

Examples:

For what is called a solecism is nothing else than the putting of words together according to a different rule from that which those of our predecessors who spoke with any authority followed. —St. Augustine, *On Christian Doctrine*

Sometimes, words being my trade, I recite to myself particularly felicitous phrases from yesterday's composition, pausing sometimes to consider a possible solecism, repeating the whole phrase, louder, when rhythm, cadence and meaning are all harmonious; and if I chance to meet acquaintances as I strut down the lane, or for that matter perfect strangers, I am quite likely to repeat the performance for them. —Jan Morristhe, "Speak Thyself," *The Wall Street Journal*, April 3, 2008

Synonyms for *solecism* include *absurdity, barbarism, blunder, faux pas, impropriety, incongruity,* and *inconsistency.*

(112) **solipsistic**
/ (ˌsälip'sistik)/

adjective

- Of or relating to solipsism, the belief or proposition that the person entertaining it alone exists and that other people exist only as ideas in his or her mind.

Examples:

Reality TV provides a daily diet of outrage in all its forms. There is the Bridezilla's furious blast of solipsistic entitlement; the boozy pettiness of Real Housewives everywhere; the bully-boy bellowing of celebrity chefs and dysfunctional-family-business bosses; the jilted scorn of lovers dismayed that their made-for-TV beaus aren't reliable. —Eric Felten, "Where Is the Outrage?" *The Wall Street Journal*, July 16, 2010

Those who understand the psyche of the comic know that many are neurotic, depressed, cynical types who find it difficult to function in the mainstream. . . . We often have narcissistic or even solipsistic personalities; demanding approval from total strangers on a nightly basis in the form of concerted laughter. —Bruce Clark, "Do You Have to Be Depressed to Be Funny?" *The Huffington Post*, June 14, 2010

[Sara Maitland's *A Book of Silence*] is a strikingly refreshing book to read, in the midst of the clamor and din, ever-mounting distraction, yelling TV pundits, **solipsistic** tweeting, and flash-card sentiment of our Internet age. —Julia Baird, "The Devil Loves Cell Phones," *Newsweek*, October 22, 2009

Solipsistic comes from the Latin words *sōlus,* meaning "alone," and *ipse,* meaning "self."

113

soporific
/ (sop͵ə-rif'ik *or* sō͵pə-rif'ik)/

adjective
• Tending to produce sleep.

noun
• Anything that causes sleep, as certain medicines.

Examples:
As it happens, milk contains a benzodiazepine-like substance, which could account for its legendary **soporific** effect. —Jennifer LaRue Huget, "Eat, Drink and Be Healthy," *The Washington Post*, July 29, 2010

The overly warm classroom and Professor Johnson's low droning voice created such a **soporific** atmosphere that at least one student fell asleep every week. —Wordnik

For O'Brien, in the soporific culture of mid-twentieth-century Ireland, the novel itself is a kind of sleep, a way of being neither dead nor alive and thus of drawing energy from entropy. —Fintan O'Toole, "Oblomov in Dublin," *The New York Review of Books*, August 13, 2009

Fumiyo Ikeda was for many years a dancer with Anne Teresa De Keersmaeker's Rosas company, and in the solo work In Pieces, created with writer Tim Etchells, she presents us with an hour-long performance of, by turns, exquisite insight and soporific dullness. —Luke Jennings, "Cruel; In Pieces," *The Guardian*, July 4, 2010

Soporific comes from the Latin word *sopor,* meaning "deep sleep."

specious
(114)
/ (spē'shəs)/

adjective

1 Pleasing to the eye; externally fair or showy; appearing beautiful or charming; sightly; beautiful.
2 Superficially fair, just, or correct; appearing well; apparently right; plausible; beguiling.
3 Appearing actual, or in reality; actually existing; not imaginary.

Examples:

They had not the effrontery to wrap up their motives in **specious** expressions of concern for my health, but stated their
point of view with brutal frankness, as is their wont. —Ian
Hay, *The Right Stuff*, 1912

This is from Kate Strong: now if there is a girl in the world
for whom I cherish an aversion, it is Katie Strong! She is
what I call a **specious** pig, and why she wanted to send me a
Christmas card I simply can't imagine. We were on terms of
undying hatred. —Mrs. George de Horne Vaizey, *About Peggy Saville*,
1900

Trying to connect that long ago Racine club with the present Super Bowl contender is an exercise in **specious** geneal-
ogy. A professional sports team is a fluid concept, defined
neither by its management or home town, nor by its insig-
nias or players. —Richard B. Woodward, "What's in a Name: The Folly
of Being a Loyal Pro Sports Fan," *The Huffington Post*, January 30, 2009

Specious has the connotations of seeming to be true—often too good
to be true—but something that is *specious* is actually *fallacious*, "de-
ceptive, misleading."

115 **supercilious**

/ (sōō͵pər-sil'ē-əs)/

adjective

1 Lofty with pride; haughtily contemptuous; overbearing.

2 Manifesting haughtiness or proceeding from it; overbearing; arrogant: as a *supercilious* air; *supercilious* behavior.

Examples:

And there, not a dozen paces from her, was Maxwell Wyndham, carelessly approaching, his hands in his pockets, his hat thrust to the back of his head, a faint, **supercilious** smile cocking one corner of his mouth, his whole bearing one of elaborate unconsciousness. —Ethel M. Dell, *The Keeper of the Door*, 1915

"A poodle," Florence corrected her, and then turned to Herbert in **supercilious** astonishment. "A French Poodle! My goodness! I should think you were old enough to know that much, anyway—goin' on fourteen years old!" —Booth Tarkington, *Gentle Julia*, 1922

The problem was that Bush had been himself. Not the playful, warm man he could be, but the peevish, hyper man he also was. . . . His whole body and manner cried out that he was a president with a war to fight who didn't want to be bothered trading verbal jabs with the kind of **supercilious**

147

know-it-all he had loathed since Yale days. —Holly Bailey et al., "Talking the Talk," *Newsweek*, November 15, 2003

Supercilious comes from the Latin word *supercilium*, meaning "pride." *Supercilium* means literally "eyebrow," as in raising one's eyebrow in haughtiness or pride.

116

taciturn
/ (tas'i-tûrn,)/

adjective
- Silent or reserved in speech; saying little; not inclined to speak or converse.

Examples:
He turned around and eyed the doctor, who stood in taciturn silence. —E. Phillips Oppenheim, *The Vanished Messenger*, 1914

Mr Ward was again taciturn as before. He felt that, as a city man, he was among people who knew him, and lest he should be overheard he was habitually silent. —William Henry Giles Kingston, *My First Voyage to Southern Seas*, 1876

Khadr, normally taciturn or distracted in court, smiled at a panel of military officers and said "How are you?" after his military defense lawyer introduced him. —Peter Finn, "Sentencing of Detainee Stalls at Guantanamo," *The Washington Post*, August 10, 2010

They were sharply contrasting characters, Barnes somewhat dour and **taciturn**, Paul exuberant and cavalier, both on the pitch and off it. —Brian Glanville, "Ken Barnes Obituary," *The Guardian*, July 14, 2010

While some of Cromer's actors play their New England **taciturn** behavior a little too subtly, in the end, we find the power of Wilder's work coheres precisely because less becomes more. —Brad Schreiber, "Let Me Off at Off- and Off-Off-Broadway," *The Huffington Post*, November 1, 2009

Synonyms for *taciturn* include *dumb*, *mute*, *reserved*, *reticent*, *silent*, and *uncommunicative*.

(117) **tautology**
/ (tô-tol'ə-jē)/

noun

1 Repetition of the same word, or use of several words conveying the same idea, in the same immediate context.

2 The repetition of the same thing in different words; the useless repetition of the same idea or meaning.

3 A statement that is true for all values of its variables.

Examples:

The unnecessary repetition of words or phrases occurs in his greatest works, while in the later, the polemical, writings, it has become greatly exaggerated. . . . One must think that this **tautology** is deliberate on the author's part, since he is never in haste to publish uncorrected matter; but the result is harshness, which increases with every fresh work. —Isabel F. Hapgood, *Tolstoy's "Kreutzer Sonata,"* 1890

We should likewise be aware of **tautology**, which is a repetition of the same word or thought, or the use of many similar words or thoughts. —Grenville Kleiser, *The Training of a Public Speaker*, 1920

This unmanly dread of simplicity, and of what is called "**tautology**," gives rise to a patchwork made up of scraps of poetic quotations, unmeaning periphrases, and would-be humorous circumlocutions,—a style of all styles perhaps the most objectionable and offensive, which may be known and avoided by the name of Fine Writing. —Edwin Abbott Abbott, *How to Write Clearly*, 1883

Tautology is from the Greek word *tautologos*, meaning "redundant."

118 **trammel**
/ (tram'əl)/

noun

1 A net for fishing.

2 A kind of shackle used to make a horse amble.

3 Whatever hinders activity, freedom, or progress; an impediment.

verb
1 To catch as in a net.
2 To shackle.
3 To train slavishly; inure to conformity or obedience.

Examples:
From all which it is, I think, manifest that the men who framed these documents, desirous above all things of cutting themselves and their people loose from every kind of **trammel**, still felt the necessity of enforcing religion—of making it, to a certain extent, a matter of State duty. —Anthony Trollope, *North America*, 1862

This would also help to keep our armed forces out of the clutches of the "European Union" as presently constituted which must **trammel** their independence if it is to completely destroy our sovereignty. —David Blackburn, "The Tories May Raid the Aid Budget to Fund the Military," *Spectator*, January 15, 2010

There is no doubt that the government has the right to expropriate land that is needed for the Games. But when it exercises that right, it must do so in a way that doesn't **trammel** the rights of those concerned. —Jane Buchanan, "Don't

Trample the Olympic Ideals in Russia," *The Wall Street Journal*, May 25, 2009

Trammel comes from the Latin word *trēmaculum: trēs*, "three," and *macula*, "mesh."

119

vertiginous
/ (vər-tij'ə-nəs)/

adjective
1 Turning around; whirling; rotary: as a *vertiginous* motion.
2 Affected with vertigo; giddy; dizzy.
3 Apt to turn or change; unstable.
4 Apt to make one giddy; inducing giddiness: as a *vertiginous* height.

Examples:
Reminiscent of the Mediterranean, centuries-old olive groves are built in vertiginous terraces with honey-coloured limestone walls. —Joanna Blythman, "Farming in Palestine," *The Guardian*, September 13, 2009

Fashionistas in vertiginous heels followed the models out into the street and curious passers-by snapping cell phone pictures jostled for a spot on the sidewalk as faux police officers tried to keep a lid on it all. —Jenny Barchfield, "Kenzo Makes a Catwalk of Paris' Streets," *The China Post*, January 25, 2010

The film, directed by Mike Mitchell, has its intermittent pleasures: toy-like landscapes in enchanting colors; the mysterious charm of Mr. Banderas's delivery, which gets laughs from every line; a witches' ball, followed by the witches' **vertiginous** pursuit of Shrek through the 3-D spaces of a palace.
—"Even with a Third Dimension, 'Shrek Forever After' Is a Little Thin," *The Wall Street Journal*, June 18, 2010

Vertiginous comes from the Latin word *vertīgō*, meaning "a whirling." *Vertigo* is a condition in which a person or surrounding objects appear to be whirling about.

(120) **wrought**
/ (rôt)/

adjective
- Worked, as distinguished from rough: as in masonry, carpentry, etc.

Examples:
In Lecce, balconies adorned in **wrought** iron hug narrow streets; the facades of churches are decorated with images of saints and beasts, fluted columns and baroque evocations hewn in the soft, yellowish rock known as pietra leccese. —Joel Weickgenant, "Puglia's Fiery Pizzica," *The Wall Street Journal*, August 13, 2010

His relish for humor and for the study of character, as we have before observed, brought him often into convivial company of a vulgar kind; but he discriminated between their vulgarity and their amusing qualities, or rather **wrought** from the whole those familiar features of life which form the staple of his most popular writings. —Washington Irving, *The Life of Oliver Goldsmith*, 1897

The hotel sits on a riverbank in Moscow about 10 minutes from the spot where Boris Yeltsin once stood defiantly upon a tank, setting in train the second Russian revolution. What that revolution has **wrought** is now on display, in surreal fashion, every day in the hotel's lobby. —Bill Powell, "Murder in Moscow," *Newsweek*, November 25, 1996

Wrought means "worked," and *overwrought* means "worked too hard or too much; elaborate; overdone."